GA HOUSES 100号記念

〈日本〉と〈海外〉，戦後から現代に至るまでの住宅建築の流れを紹介します。2冊合わせて〈世界の住宅〉を俯瞰する特集号です

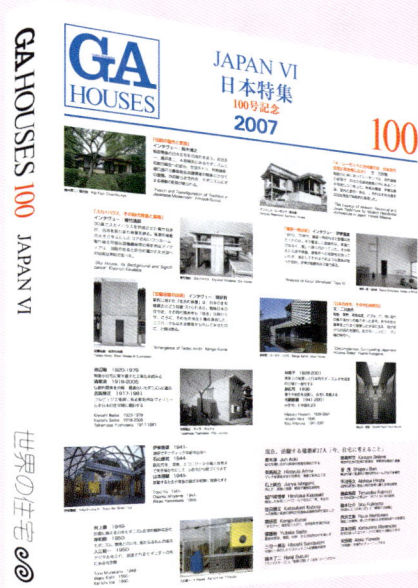

288 pages, 124 in color
¥2,848

100
100号記念第一弾
JAPAN VI
日本特集 2007

「伝統の融合と変容～日本藝術院会員による住宅の時代とその前史」　鈴木博之
「A・レーモンドと吉村順三は，日本近代住宅に何を残したか」　三沢浩
「スカイハウス，その時代背景と意味」　菊竹清訓
「篠原一男分析」　伊東豊雄
「安藤忠雄の出現」　隈研吾
「日本の住宅，その今日的状況」　二川由夫

戦後住宅年表

"*Fusion and Transfiguration of Tradition in Japanese Modernism*" Hiroyuki Suzuki
"*The Legacy of Antonin Raymond and Junzo Yoshimura for Modern Residential Architecture in Japan*" Hiroshi Misawa
"*Sky House, its Background and Significance*" Kiyonori Kikutake
"*Analysis on Kazuo Shinohara*" Toyo Ito
"*Emergence of Tadao Ando*" Kengo Kuma
"*Circumstances Surrounding Japanese Houses Today*" Yoshio Futagawa

Chronological Table of Houses 1945-2007

The Architect who Led in the Times after WWII
〈時代をつくった建築家たち〉
Antonin Raymond (1888-1976), Junzo Yoshimura (1908-1997), Kiyoshi Ikebe (1920-1979), Kiyoshi Seike (1918-2005), Takamasa Yoshizaka (1917-1981), Kazuo Shinohara (1925-2006), Masako Hayashi (1928-2001), Kiyoshi Kikutake (1928-), Hiroshi Hara (1936-), Tadao Ando (1941-), Kiko Mozuna (1941-2001), Toyo Ito (1941-), Osamu Ishiyama (1944-), Riken Yamamoto (1945-), Toru Murakami (1949-), Waro Kishi (1950-), Kei'ichi Irie (1950-)

Interview with 17 Architects at the Forefront of Residential Design
〈現在活躍する建築家17人「今，何を考えて住宅をつくるのか」〉
Jun Aoki, Hiroyuki Arima, Junya Ishigami, Hirotaka Kidosaki, Katsufumi Kubota, Kengo Kuma, Yutaka Saito, Hiroshi Sambuichi, Ryoji Suzuki, Kazuyo Sejima, Shigeru Ban, Akihisa Hirata, Terunobu Fujimori, Sou Fujimoto, Ryue Nishizawa, Katsuhiro Miyamoto, Akira Yoneda

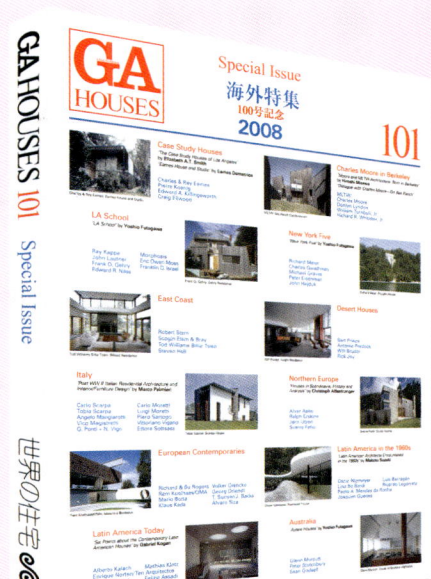

352 pages, 192 in color
¥3,600

101
100号記念第二弾
Special Issue
海外特集 2008

アメリカ西部
「ロサンゼルスのケース・スタディ・ハウス」　エリザベス・A・T・スミス
「イームズ・ハウスのこと」　イームズ・デメトリアス
「バークレーで生まれたムーアとMLTW建築」　三沢浩
「チャールズ・ムーアとの対話——シーランチをめぐって」　チャールズ・ムーア，二川幸夫
「LAスクール」　二川由夫
アメリカ東部　「ニューヨーク・ファイブ」　二川由夫
イタリア　「第二次大戦後のイタリア住宅建築とインテリア・家具デザイン」　マルコ・パルミエーリ
北欧　「北欧の住宅，その背景と分析」　クリストフ・アッフェントランガー
中南米——1960年代と現代
「60年代，中南米で出会った人たち」　鈴木恂，二川幸夫
「ラテンアメリカの現代住宅について，6つのポイント」　ガブリエル・コーガン
オーストラリア　「オージー・ハウス」　二川由夫

全96作品掲載

West Coast
"*The Case Study Houses of Los Angeles*" Elizabeth A.T. Smith
"*Eames House and Studio*" Eames Demetrios
"*Moore and MLTW Architecture, Born in Berkeley*" Hiroshi Misawa
"*Dialogue with Charles Moore—On Sea Ranch*"
"*LA School*" Yoshio Futagawa
East Coast "*New York Five*" Yoshio Futagawa
Italy "*Post WW II Italian Residential Architecture and Interior/Furniture Design*" Marco Palmieri
Northern Europe "*Houses in Scandinavia, History and Analysis*" Christoph Affentranger
Latin America in the 1960s and Today
"*Latin American Architects Encountered in the 1960s*" Makoto Suzuki and Yukio Futagawa
"*Six Points about the Contemporary Latin American Houses*" Gabriel Kogan
Australia "*Aussie Houses*" Yoshio Futagawa

96 works are included in total

表記価格に消費税は含まれておりません。

GA Contemporary Architecture

For the past thirty years, our basic attitude has remained the same. On-site reportages from around the world have amassed a vast collection of architectural works. For this brand-new series of publication, masterpieces of contemporary architecture would be selected from our extensive archives to be classified into various types of building such as museum, library, theater, university, office, laboratory, and sports, commercial or transportation facilities. A compilation recording the paths of contemporary architecture for the time to come.

30余年にわたり行ってきました，当社の一貫した基本姿勢である現地取材によって蓄積された膨大な建築作品のアーカイブから，厳選した現代建築の名作を，美術・博物館，図書館，劇場，大学，スポーツ，商業，交通，オフィス・研究所……といったビルディング・タイプごとに分類し，再集成いたします。
未来に向けて，現代建築を記録するシリーズです。

Japanese and English text
Size: 300×228mm

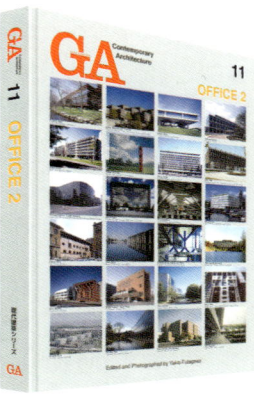

新刊
304 total pages, 136 in color ¥5,700

11 OFFICE 2

SOM Connecticut General Life Insurance Company Headquarters; **Minoru Yamasaki** Reynolds Metals Company, Sales Office; **Mies van der Rohe** Bacardi Office; **Alvar Aalto** Enso-Gutzeit Company Headquarters; **Eero Saarinen and others** Deere and Company Headquarters; **K. Roche, J. Dinkeloo** Union Carbide Corporation World Headquarters; **Herman Hertzberger** Centraal Beheer Office; **Gunnar Birkerts** Federal Reserve Bank of Minneapolis; **Oscar Niemeyer** Mondadori Building; **Harry Seidler** Trade Group Office, Canberra; **Carlo Scarpa** Banca Popolare di Verona; **Norman Foster** Willis Faber & Dumas Headquarters; **Manteola and others** Buenos Aires Color Television Production Center; **Hiroshi Hara** Yamato International Inc. Tokyo Branch; **James Stirling** Braun Headquarters; **Arata Isozaki** Team Disney Building; **Legorreta Arquitectos** IBM Southlake and Village Center; **Tadao Ando** Raika Headquarters; **Richard Meier** Canal+ Television Headquarters; **Eric O. Moss** Pittard Sullivan; **Richard Rogers** Channel 4 Television Headquarters; **Ten Arquitectos** Televisa Mixed Use Building, Mexico City; **Steven Holl** Sarphatistraat Offices; **Meyer en van Schooten** ING Group Headquarters; **Morphosis** Hypo Alpe-Adria Bank Headquarters; **Frank O. Gehry** IAC Building; **Jean Nouvel** Brembo's Research and Development Center

54 works are collected in total.

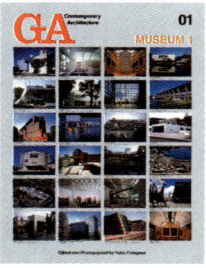

01 MUSEUM 1

Junzo Sakakura Museum of Modern Art, Kamakura; **K. Roche J. Dinkeloo** Oakland Museum; **Mies van der Rohe** New National Gallery, Berlin; **Louis I. Kahn** Kimbell Art Museum; **James Stirling, Michael Wilford** Staatsgalerie Extension and New Chamber Theater; **Yoshio Taniguchi** Ken Domon Museum of Photography; **Frank O. Gehry** California Aerospace Museum and Theater; **Toyo Ito** Yatsushiro Municipal Museum; **Sverre Fehn** Glacier Museum; **Balkrishna V. Doshi** Hussain-Doshi Gufa Museum; **Jean Nouvel** Cartier Foundation; **Peter Zumthor** Art Museum, Bregenz; **Tadao Ando** Naoshima Contemporary Art Museum; **Steven Holl** KIASMA Museum of Contemporary Art; **K. Sejima + R. Nishizawa** O-Museum; **Herzog & de Meuron** Tate Modern
50 works are collected in total.

336 total pages, 136 in color ¥5,700

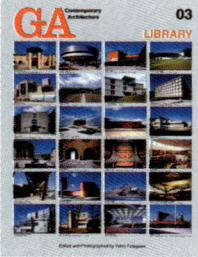

03 LIBRARY

SOM Beinecke Rare Book and Manuscript Library, Yale University; **Louis I. Kahn** Exeter Library, Phillips Exeter Academy; **Paul Rudolph** Niagara Falls Public Library; **Gunnar Birkerts** Tougaloo College Library; **Hans Scharoun** Berlin State Library; **Arata Isozaki** Kitakyushu Central Library; **Dominique Perrault** Bibliothèque Nationale de France; **Álvaro Siza** Main Library, University of Aveiro; **William Bruder + DWL** Phoenix Central Library; **Scogin Elam and Bray** Ross-Blakley Law Library, Arizona State University; **Legorreta Arquitectos** South Chula Vista Library; **Mecanoo** Library of Delft University of Technology; **Mansilla + Tuñón** Madrid Regional Documentary Center; **Hiroshi Hara** Miyagi Prefectural Library; **Toyo Ito** Sendai Mediatheque; **OMA** Seattle Central Library
50 works are collected in total.

320 total pages, 152 in color ¥5,700

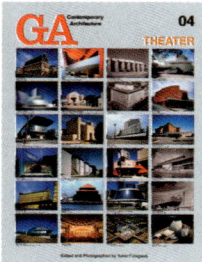

04 THEATER

Frank L. Wright Dallas Theater Center; **Alvar Aalto** House of Culture; **Hans Scharoun** Berlin Philharmonic Hall; **Kunio Maekawa** Kyoto Kaikan; **Jørn Utzon** Sydney Opera House; **Antonin Raymond** Gunma Music Center; **John M. Johansen** Oklahoma Theater Center; **Frank O. Gehry** Walt Disney Concert Hall; **Rafael Viñoly** Tokyo International Forum; **Rafael Moneo** Kursaal Auditorium and Congress Center; **Santiago Calatrava** Auditorio de Tenerife; **Kengo Kuma** Noh Stage in the Forest; **Coop Himmelblau** UFA Cinema Center Dresden; **Bolles-Wilson** Luxor Theater Rotterdam; **Bernard Tschumi** Zenith de Rouen; **Christian de Portzamparc** Luxembourg Philharmonie; **OMA** Casa da Música; **Toyo Ito** Matsumoto Performing Arts Centre
43 works are collected in total.

320 total pages, 144 in color ¥5,700

05 UNIVERSITY

Mies van der Rohe Crown Hall, Illinois Institute of Technology; **Alvar Aalto** Auditorium and Main Building, Power Plant, Helsinki University of Technology; **Paul Rudolph** Art and Architecture Building, Yale University; **Le Corbusier** Carpenter Center, Harvard University; **Louis I. Kahn** Indian Institute of Management; **Craig Ellwood** Hillside Campus, Art Center College of Design; **Álvaro Siza** Faculty of Architecture, University of Porto; **Norman Foster** Faculty of Law, University of Cambridge; **Legorreta Arquitectos** National Center of the Arts, Mexico City; **OMA** Educatorium, Utrecht University; **Bernard Tschumi** Alfred Lerner Hall, Columbia University; **Riken Yamamoto** Saitama Prefectural University; **Frank O. Gehry** Ray and Maria Stata Center
48 works are collected in total.

336 total pages, 152 in color ¥5,700

表記価格に消費税は含まれておりません。

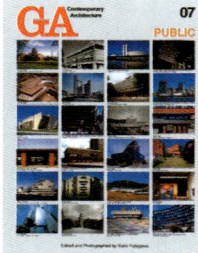

07 PUBLIC

Oscar Niemeyer and others Ministry of Education and Health; **Le Corbusier** Chandigarh; **Marcel Breuer and others** UNESCO Headquarters; **Oscar Niemeyer, Lúcio Costa** Brasilia; **Kenzo Tange** Kagawa Prefectural Government Office; **Frank L. Wright, Aaron Green** Marin County Civic Center; **Zvi Hecker, Alfred Neumann, Eldar Sharon** Bat Yam Town Hall; **Viljo Revell** Toronto City Hall; **C. F. Murphy Associates with SOM** Chicago Civic Center; **Louis I. Kahn** Bangladesh Parliament; **Zaha Hadid** Vitra Fire Station; **Toyo Ito** Yatsushiro Fire Station; **Arata Isozaki** Okayama-nishi Police Station; **Christian de Portzamparc** Courts of Justice, Grasse; **Jean Nouvel** Courts of Justice, Nantés; **Riken Yamamoto** Nishi Fire Station, Hiroshima; **OMA** Netherlands Embassy Berlin
46 works are collected in total.

320 total pages, 152 in color ¥5,700

08 TRANSPORTATION

Eero Saarinen JFK International Airport, TWA Terminal; **Pier L. Nervi** George Washington Bridge Bus Station; **HOK** Dallas/Fort Worth International Airport; **Murphy/Jahn** Chicago O'Hare International Airport; **Norman Foster** Stansted Airport, Terminal Zone; **Ricard Bofill** Barcelona Airport; **Nicholas Grimshaw** Waterloo International Terminal; **SNCF** Lille Europe Station; **Renzo Piano** Kansai International Airport; **Santiago Calatrava** TGV Station, Lyon-Satolas Airport; **Paul Andreu** Charles de Gaulle, Terminal 2, Hall F; **Hiroshi Hara** Kyoto Station; **Norman Foster** Hong Kong International Airport; **Santiago Calatrava** Orient Station, Lisbon; **Foreign Office Architects** Yokohama International Passenger Terminal; **Zaha Hadid** Car Park and Terminus Hoenheim-Nord; **SANAA** Marine Station Naoshima
43 works are collected in total.

288 total pages, 124 in color ¥5,700

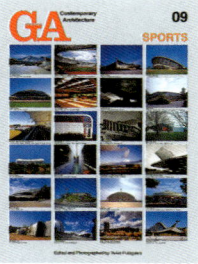

09 SPORTS

Matthew Nowicki J. S. Dorton Arena; **Paulo M. da Rocha** Sports Hall of Club Atlético Paulistano; **Pier L. Nervi** Small/Large Sports Palace, Rome; **Kenzo Tange** Yoyogi National Gymnasium; **SOM** Oakland-Alameda County Coliseum, **Félix Candela** Sports Palace, Mexico City; **Günter Behnisch** Sports Hall, Auf dem Schäfersfeld; **Fumihiko Maki** Tokyo Metropolitan Gymnasium; **Renzo Piano** San Nicola Stadium; **Enric Miralles** National Center for Rhythmic Gymnastics; **Dominique Perrault** Olympic Velodrome and Swimming Hall; **Hiroshi Hara:** Sapporo Dome; **Norman Foster** Wembley National Stadium; **Zaha Hadid** Bergisel Ski Jump; **Morphosis** University of Cincinnati Campus Recreation Center; **Eduardo Souto de Moura** Braga Stadium; **Herzog & de Meuron** Allianz Arena
50 works are collected in total.

288 total pages, 128 in color ¥5,700

10 OFFICE 1

Harrison and Abramovitz Alcoa Headquarters Pittsburgh; **SOM** Lever House; **Frank L. Wright** Price Tower; **Gio Ponti and others** Pirelli Tower; **Walter Gropius and others** PanAm Building; **Eero Saarinen** CBS Headquarters; **Minoru Yamasaki** World Trade Center; **K. Roche, J. Dinkeloo** Ford Foundation Headquarters; **I. M. Pei** Christian Science Center; **Egon Eiermann** Olivetti German Headquarters; **Johnson/Burgee** Pennzoil Place; **Edward L. Barnes** IBM Tower New York; **Murphy/Jahn** Xerox Center; **Richard Rogers** Lloyd's of London; **KPF** 333 Wacker Drive; **Norman Foster** Hongkong and Shanghai Banking Corporation Headquarters; **Michael Graves** Humana Building; **Hiroshi Hara** Umeda Sky Building; **Renzo Piano** Aurora Place; **Norman Foster** 30 St Mary Axe; **Jean Nouvel** Torre Agba
59 works are collected in total.

280 total pages, 144 in color ¥5,700

94 最新刊

特別レポート：ブラジルの現在
記事：「ニーマイヤーとシザの対談から」二川由夫，
「ブラジル・モダン，もう一つの源泉」斎藤日登美
作品：磯崎新＋KAJIMA DESIGN ハラ ミュージアム アーク
小嶋一浩＋赤松佳珠子／CAt＋アルパック／とどろみの森学園 箕面市立止々呂美小学校・中学校
高松伸／丸美産業本社屋
安藤忠雄＋東京急行電鉄＋日建設計＋東急設計コンサルタント／東急東横線渋谷駅
PROJECT：磯崎新／New Bologna Central Station
SANAA Multifunctional Building of The Serralves Foundation
隈研吾／Iskandar Iconic Park
PLOT：「新UCバークレー美術館／パシフィック・フィルムアーカイブ」編
設計：伊東豊雄／phase 1：初期スタディ
「ROLEX ラーニング・センター」編 設計：SANAA／phase 0：創造過程
「K MUSEUM」編 設計：北川原温／phase 1：基本設計へ繋がるスタディ
「(仮称) ナミックス・テクノコア」編 設計：山本理顕／phase 2：形と直結した構造設計のプロセス
連載：「GA日記」二川幸夫
GA広場：「シニシズムを越えたユートピア」石山修武，「本の実態感と建築的物質感のバランス」
金沢市西部図書館，堀場弘，「木の万能性 部分と全体」Final Wooden House，藤本壮介，
「井桁状の壁で13部屋をスタックする」カタガラスの家／TNA＋満田衛資，「空間に浮遊した音と光の地形」〈風鈴〉伊東豊雄＋takram
160 pages, 96 in color ¥2,333

93

新 現代建築を考える○と×
「福生市庁舎」
座談会：山本理顕・内藤廣・二川幸夫
特集：くまもとアートポリス・リローデッド
インタビュー：伊東豊雄
佐藤光彦／熊本駅西口駅前広場，藤本壮介／八代世代モクバン，渡瀬正記・永吉歩／Wooden Lace，西沢立衛／熊本駅東口駅前広場（暫定形），アトリエ・アンド・アイ＋坂本一成／宇土市立網津小学校
作品：隈研吾＋NTTファシリティーズ／朝日放送
山本理顕／福生市庁舎 ザハ・ハディド／モバイル・アート シャネル コンテンポラリー アート コンテイナー
PLOT：
宇土市立宇土小学校，小嶋一浩＋赤松佳珠子，ヨコミゾマコト，山中新太郎，小野田泰明
長岡市シティホール／隈研吾
ナミックス・テクノコア（仮称）／山本理顕
杉並区立杉並芸術館／伊東豊雄
GA広場：「固定化ではなく，多様さを刺激する」OMA／AMO，「建築を風景化させるとは」石上純也＋西沢立衛，「散歩のような建築」日建設計，「屋根をアクティビティのベースにする」宮本佳明，他
160 pages, 80 in color ¥2,333

92

新 現代建築を考える○と×
「東京大学 情報学環・福武ホール」
座談会：安藤忠雄・石山修武・二川幸夫
特集：［さけて通れないコルビュジエ］
第3回「ユルバニスムと都市計画」
磯崎新 隈研吾 キラン・ジョシ 横山禎徳
髙間三郎
作品：安藤忠雄／東京大学 情報学環・福武ホール 西沢立衛／十和田市現代美術館 三分一博志／犬島アートプロジェクト「精錬所」 隈研吾／料亭開花亭 別館「sou-an」，Sake no hana
記事：「建築と悪戦苦闘する」安藤忠雄，「アート・建築・都市が同時に起きる」西沢立衛，「産業遺産と離島プロジェクト」三分一博志，「新旧を共鳴させる三層の組格子」「等価な価値を生む木造のオネスティ」隈研吾
PLOT：台湾大学新社会科学院棟／伊東豊雄
武蔵野美術大学美術資料図書館／藤本壮介
豊田市生涯学習センター逢妻交流館／妹島和世
GA広場：「多国籍なアクティビティを建築化する」CAt＋CAn，「寡黙なヴォリュームに穿つ無数の穴」下吹越武人，「自己生成させた三次曲面の床」伊東豊雄，他
168 pages, 96 in color ¥2,333

91

特集：［さけて通れないコルビュジエ］
第2回「ロンシャンとラ・トゥーレット」
「終わりであり，始まりである」磯崎新
「ガラスの箱とロンシャン」原広司
「原理を応用する難しさ」隈研吾
「建築をつくることにとっての原点の大切さ」横文彦
「著述家としての建築家」井上章一
作品：
磯崎新／深圳文化中心
隈研吾／呉市音戸市民センター
石上純也／神奈川工科大学KAIT工房
山口隆／Silent Office
日建設計＋十村工藝社＋大林組／乃村工藝社本社ビル
プロジェクト：伊東豊雄／SUMIKA Project by Tokyo gas（Ⅰ・パヴィリオン）
PLOT：
湯町地区観光交流センター（仮称）／隈研吾
武蔵野美術大学美術資料図書館／藤本壮介
日立駅自由通路及び橋上駅舎／妹島和世
GA広場：「〈換喩〉のランドスケープ」ザハ・ハディド，「建築を感覚とリンクさせる」フィリップスデザイン［プローブ］プロジェクト／編集部，「ファブリック・裁断・振る舞い」石上純也，「自分が居る場所と，そうでない場所の釣り合い」永山祐子，他
160 pages, 88 in color ¥2,333

90

新 現代建築を考える○と×
「ニューミュージアム」
座談会：妹島和世・西沢立衛・小嶋一浩・二川由夫
対談：［総括と展望・続編］建築2007／2008
山本理顕・二川幸夫
特集：［さけて通れないコルビュジエ］
第1回「住宅，初期のコンセプトについて」
鈴木恂／入江経一／月尾嘉男／佐々木睦朗／鈴木了二／平田晃久／米田明／隈研吾／林美佐／西沢立衛／青木淳／千代章一郎／伊東豊雄
作品：妹島和世＋西沢立衛／SANAA／ニューミュージアム 横文彦／三原市芸術文化センター ポポロ 澤岡清秀＋山本圭介・堀啓二／工学院大学八王子キャンパス ステューデントセンター MVRDV／GYRE
PLOT：台中メトロポリタン・オペラハウス Catenoid と Plug によって Emerging Grid を実現する／伊東豊雄
GA広場：「町の出来事と室内の出来事の間」西沢立衛，「広場にかかる雲」西沢立衛，「超極薄繊維の布を浮かせた茶室」隈研吾，「1トンの箱を浮かせるには」佐藤淳，「約300本のフラットバーで屋根荷重を支える」小西泰孝，「まちに開かれた〈中土間〉」隈研吾建築都市設計事務所
176 pages, 88 in color ¥2,333

0Key to Abbreviations

ALC	alcove
ARCD	arcade/covered passageway
ART	art room
ATL	atelier
ATR	atrium
ATT	attic
AV	audio-visual room
BAL	balcony
BAR	bar
BK	breakfast room
BR	bedroom
BRG	bridge/catwalk
BTH	bathroom
BVD	belvedere/lookout
CAR	carport/car shelter
CH	children's room
CEL	cellar
CL	closet/walk-in closet
CLK	cloak
CT	court
D	dining room
DEN	den
DK	deck
DN	stairs-down
DRK	darkroom
DRS	dressing room/wardrobe
DRW	drawing room
E	entry
ECT	entrance court
EH	entrance hall
EV	elevator
EXC	exercise room
F	family room
FPL	fireplace
FYR	foyer
GAL	gallery
GDN	garden
GRG	garage
GRN	greenhouse
GST	guest room/guest bedroom
GZBO	gazebo
H	hall
ING	inglenook
K	kitchen
L	living room
LBR	library
LBY	lobby
LDRY	laundry
LFT	loft
LGA	loggia
LGE	lounge
LWL	light well
MAID	maid room
MBR	master bedroom
MBTH	master bathroom
MECH	mechanical
MLTP	multipurpose room
MSIC	music room
MUD	mud room
OF	office
P	porch/portico
PAN	pantry/larder
PLY	playroom
POOL	swimming pool/pool/pond
PT	patio
RE	rear entry
RT	roof terrace
SHW	shower
SIT	sitting room
SHOP	shop
SKY	skylight
SL	slope/ramp
SLP	sleeping loft
SNA	sauna
STD	studio
STDY	study
ST	staircase/stair hall
STR	storage/storeroom
SUN	sunroom/sun parlor/solarium
SVE	service entry
SVYD	service yard
TAT	tatami room/tea ceremony room
TER	terrace
UP	stairs-up
UTL	utility room
VD	void/open
VRA	veranda
VSTB	vestibule
WC	water closet
WRK	workshop/work room

表記価格に消費税は含まれておりません。

Global Architecture
GA HOUSES

A.D.A. EDITA Tokyo

106

目次	Contents
ブラジル特集	**Special Feature: Brazil**
文:「ブラジルのモダニズム建築」 8 二川由夫	Essay: 'Modernism Architecture of Brazil' Yoshio Futagawa
巨匠の住宅:パウロ・メンデス・ダ・ローシャ 10 自邸, ブラジル, サン・パウロ	Residential Masterpieces: Paulo Mendes da Rocha Architect's House, São Paulo, Brazil
編集長インタビュー 32 アンジェロ・ブッチ／SPBRアルキテートス	**A DIALOGUE WITH EDITOR** Angelo Bucci/SPBR Arquitetos
SPBRアルキテートス リオ・デ・ジャネイロの家 38 カラピキュイバの家 60	**SPBR Arquitetos** House in Rio de Janeiro House in Carapicuiba
アンドラード／モレティン 76 ハウスRR	**Andrade Morettin** House RR

《世界の住宅》106
発行：二川幸夫
編集：二川由夫

2008年 8月25日発行
エーディーエー・エディタ・トーキョー
東京都渋谷区千駄ヶ谷3-12-14
電話(03)3403-1581(代)
ファクス(03)3497-0649
E-mail: info@ga-ada.co.jp
http://www.ga-ada.co.jp

ロゴタイプ・デザイン：細谷巖

印刷・製本：図書印刷株式会社

取次店
トーハン・日販・大阪屋
栗田出版販売・西村書店
中央社・太洋社

禁無断転載

ISBN978-4-87140-776-2 C1352

GA HOUSES 106
Publisher: Yukio Futagawa
Editor: Yoshio Futagawa

Published in August 2008
©A.D.A. EDITA Tokyo Co., Ltd.
3-12-14 Sendagaya, Shibuya-ku,
Tokyo, 151-0051 Japan
Tel. (03)3403-1581
Fax.(03)3497-0649
E-mail: info@ga-ada.co.jp
http://www.ga-ada.co.jp

Logotype Design: Gan Hosoya

Printed in Japan by
Tosho Printing Co., Ltd.

All rights reserved.

Copyright of Photographs:
©GA photographers

Cover: House in Rio de Janeiro
by SPBR Arquitetos
pp.4-5: aerial view of São Paulo City
Photos by Yukio Futagawa
pp.6-7: Copacabana Beach, Rio de Janeiro
Photo by Yoshio Futagawa
Copyediting and translation: Lisa Tani
(pp.32-37)
English translation: Lisa Tani (p.148),
Kei Sato (pp.8-9, p.20, p.160)
和訳：菊池泰子 (p.81, p.88, p.100, p.113, p.121, p.128), 吉村香苗 (p.41, p.60)

MMBBアルキテートス	86	**MMBB Arquitetos**
ヴィラ・ロマナの住宅＆スタジオ		Vila Romana Residence and Studio
ニーチェ・アルキテートス	98	**Nitsche Arquitetos**
イボランガの家		House in Iporanga
GESTOアンビエンタル	110	**GESTO Ambiental**
"ポウソ・アルト"の家		"Pouso Alto" House
プロクター／リフル・アーキテクツ	120	**Procter-Rihl Architects**
スライス・ハウス		Slice House
マルコス・アカヤバ	128	**Marcos Acayaba**
ミラン邸		Milan House
藤本壮介		**Sou Fujimoto**
house N	146	House N
Final Wooden House	160	Final Wooden House

Modernism Architecture of Brazil Yoshio Futagawa

ブラジルのモダニズム建築 二川由夫

During the first half of the 20th century, the modernism architecture movement proposed by those European masters including Le Corbusier began to be exported to all over the world. Europe as the originator of this movement did not allow the popularization of this movement so easily because of its cultural contexts developed throughout its long and profound history. However, among those countries in new continents formed by European immigrants including the United States, the bold possibility of this new 'ism', which was the latest movement of the days, was visualized as actual products under their enthusiasm toward assimilating various ideas during the course of their cultural maturity.

Those countries in the new continents started to produce various versions of modernism in each country based on their own natural features and the cultural background. The architecture peculiar to each country began to emerge among those countries starting from the United States that received the biggest influence from the modernism movement and became the strong driving force of its development, and to Mexico, Argentina, Chile, or Venezuela in the Central and South American continents.

Brazil is a large scale country, which has the largest territory in the South American continent, including the biggest jungle of the world, Amazon. The origin of the nation started as a Portuguese colony, but Brazil has developed a multi-cultural society by accepting immigrants from various countries such as Italy and Germany in Europe, or people emigrated from Japan. Its cultural and social coexistence of the multiple ethnicities has been achieved most democratically and wholesomely among those countries in the new continents, thus it is conceivable that such open breeding ground has lent itself to deeply establish the modernism movement to its new ground.

Throughout the periods before and after the World War II, Brazilian architecture went through some unique development conducted by the creative works of those pioneering architects such as Lucio Costa, Alfonso Reidy, Oscar Niemeyer, Vilanova Artigas, Lina Bo Bardi. The principle of the modernism was fostered and adapted to the unique, local conditions and contexts of Brazil, as if the idea of the modernism sympathized with Brazil's tropical climate and the culture of the people who reside there. Later on, a unique and original form of the architecture only found in Brazil has brought to light, which goes beyond the original modernism movement.

The military regime founded in 1964 brought a 20 years of cultural stagnancy to Brazil, but at the same time that also caused their architecture field to be isolated from the postmodernism movement that had involved all over the world at that time. Consequently Brazil has become one of the rarest countries that remain with the legitimate successors of the modernism movement, and this background strongly affected to produce today's young architects following the modernism principle among new generations.

Modernism movement of Brazil was unfolded mostly in the two major cities of Rio de Janeiro and São Paulo—the tropical paradise city of Rio de Janeiro with full of sun shine, and São Paulo, one of the foremost, largest cities in the world. Based on those two major cities as the stages with completely different characteristics of each, the modernism movement of Brazil was developed by reflecting those characteristics of each environment. Those who played the active roles in the modernism movement based on those two cities as footholds, are Oscar Niemeyer and Vilanova Artigas.

The most prominent presence among those architects who propelled the modernism architecture of Brazil was Oscar Niemeyer. He represented Brazil through his series of design produced in his native city Rio de Janeiro, and also the decisive series of architecture realized in the capital city of Brasília after the World War II. He was then to be recognized as a global level architects among others. His talent came to bloom in his youth, which drew attention of the master Corbusier when he visited Brazil. This master felt friendship to this young fellow, or he might have even felt great esteem for Niemeyer's excellent aesthetic sense. Niemeyer later on established his own unique architecture by going beyond and ahead of the modernism architecture. Being released from the orthodox architectural aesthetics of detailing found in modernistic period—such as the good quality details, proper dimensions, minute treatments and handling of building materials—Niemeyer headed for more daringly abstract, purified expressions. The criticism

20世紀前半，ル・コルビュジエをはじめとするヨーロッパの巨匠たちが提唱したモダニズム建築の運動は世界中に輸出されることになった。本家，ヨーロッパにおいては，その重厚な歴史の構築する文化的バックグラウンドによってこのムーブメントをそう簡単に大衆化に向かわせなかったが，アメリカ合衆国をはじめとする，ヨーロッパ移民による新大陸の国々においては，それらの国々が文化的成熟の途上にあるための吸収力の強さによって，当時最も今日的であったこの新しいイズムの強い可能性を可視化させていくこととなる。

特に新大陸の国々は，その風土やバックグラウンドによって様々なモダニズムをそれぞれの国に生み出すことになる。最も大きな洗礼とその後の発展の大きな原動力となるアメリカ合衆国をはじめ，メキシコ，アルゼンチン，チリ，ベネズエラなどの国々にそれぞれ独特な建築が出現する。

ブラジルは南アメリカ大陸で最大の国土を持ち，アマゾンという世界最大のジャングルを有するスケールの大きな国である。その起源はポルトガルの植民地であるが，イタリア，ドイツなどのヨーロッパ諸国から，また，日本からの移民たちによって形成される，混血文化・社会を形成してきた。多民族の文化・社会的共生は新大陸の諸国の中にあっても民主的で健全に形成されてきたものであり，このように開かれた土壌はモダニズム建築を深く根付かせることに寄与したと想像される。

戦前，戦後を通して，ルシオ・コスタ，アルフォンソ・レイディ，オスカー・ニーマイヤー，ヴィラノヴァ・アルティガス，リナ・ボ・バルディといった先駆的な建築家たちの創作によって，ブラジル建築はユニークな発展をすることとなる。そのトロピカルな風土，そこに暮らす人々の文化と共鳴するかのように，モダニズムの原理をブラジル独自の環境にローカライズさせながら育て，モダニズムの先にある，この国ならではのオリジナルな建築の姿が明らかになっていくこととなる。

64年に始まる軍事政権は，20年もの文化的な停滞をブラジルにもたらすことになるが，同時に，世界中を巻き込むポストモダンのムーブメントから建築界を隔離することとなり，結果的には今日，モダニズムの正調な系統が続く数少ない国となっているのも，昨今のモダニズム・フォロワーである若手の出現に大きく影響している。

ブラジルのモダン・ムーブメントは，主にリオ・デ・ジャネイロとサン・パウロの2大都市で展開されることになった。陽光の降り注ぐトロピカルの楽園都市であるリオ・デ・ジャネイロと世界有数の大都会サン・パウロ，性格の全く異なる大都市を舞台に，あたかもこの環境を鏡とする様な展開をしていくことになった。この2都市を拠点に活動したのがオスカー・ニーマイヤーとヴィラノヴァ・アルティガスであった。

ブラジルのモダニズム建築を大きく推進した建築家の中で最も大きな存在はオスカー・ニーマイヤーである。出身地リオ・デ・ジャネイロにおける一連の作品，そして，戦後，首都ブラジリアで実現された建築群の決定的な存在によって，この国を代表し，そして世界的な建築家となった。その才能は若く開花し，ブラジルを訪れた巨匠コルビュジエの眼にとまることとなる。巨匠はこの若き同士に友情を感じ，彼の卓越した美的センスに尊敬さえしたかもしれない。ニーマイヤーはその後，モダニズムを乗り越え，その先にある彼独自の建築を作り上げる。モダニズム時代に見て取れる良質なディテール，的確な寸法，緻密な材料，マテリアルの扱い方といった正調な建築の納め方の美学から解放されて，大胆に抽象化，純化された表現に向かっていく。現在，よく聞かれる彼の批評――ニーマイヤーは

often heard recently against him—describing him as the architect who draws a few lines—is indeed a big misunderstanding, as his design activity is made possible by his "skills of a master", achieved only after his complete assimilation of the orthodox modernism principle. Every single corner of his abstract works still maintains and acquires the precision of the spatial configuration. He continues to inspire and give courage to the architects among younger generations by creating boldly expressive works. Not only in his large scale public buildings with unrestrained and grandeur forms, but also in those gems of masterpieces crystalized as small residential buildings, he suggests the possibilities of his own architectural philosophy, which is based on his own senses free from the conventional architectural styles and languages. It appears that those younger generation architects inspired by Niemeyer are expanding their possibility by acquiring courage from the essential power radiated from the architecture of this great master.

On the contrary, Vilanova Artigas, who was working on the design based on São Paulo, was a quiet seeker of the modernism principle without favoring the exposure to the media such as architectural magazines. However, his series of works with his heart and soul acquired many young followers among later generations. While he created a large scale, bold space by utilizing a rough in-situ concrete as a main resource as if such space spokes for the disposition of Brazil, he also produced small scale residential buildings in introversive and subtle character especially well represented in the design of his private house, reflecting the localized modernism architecture based on the natural feature and the culture of Brazil. It is an unfortunate fact that his foresight, good natured and universal architecture philosophy has not been introduced outside of Brazil. Artigas taught at São Paulo University for many years to bring up many students, thus his remarkable services as an educator is also significant. The direct follower of Artigas who stood out among next generation architects was Paulo Mendes da Rocha, while he actually worked as an assistance of Artigas in São Paulo University. He took over and heightened the architectural philosophy of Artigas to a new stage, and he rendered a distinguished service to introduce the principle idea not only to Brazil but also to the world. His private house presented in this edition is one of his major works in his early period, and it is worth admiration that his essential architectural concept was already perfected in this building, which can be found in its spatial configuration, refined building dimensions and proportions, airily light and beautifully finished details, and treatment and manipulation of light. It is delightful to see that his idea is certainly handed over to today's Brazilian architects among younger generation, not only for the sake of Brazilian architecture field, but also for anyone in the world today.

The United States as the epicenter of the modernism architecture movement was also the center of the mass production even as for the modernism architecture. However, the principle of the architecture in the United States started to change around 1990; the introduction of the concept of a virtual space, the loss of interest and attention toward the modernism architecture by American people after the transformation of the social form and the notion of values, and the following stall and recession of the American construction field; on the contrary, other countries such as the ones in Central and South America, Asia, and Australia, which had used to be situated in the periphery of the cultural trend, started to break out instead of this major country, the United States.

It is possible to say that Brazilian architecture has a potential to grow as a new type of architecture differentiated and distinguished from the ones developed in the United States or in Japan. Brazil still has various social issues such as the problem of poverty, yet its wealth produced by those positive factors visible as the recent economic growth, stabilization of the political condition, maturity of the culture, and more particularly as an example that the promotion of the bio-energy as the result of its own measure to deal with the world wide energy and ecology issues, tells an effective story that the modernism architecture still contributes well to the lifestyles of Brazilian people who organize its new society by harmonizing beyond its multiple ethnicities.

At this moment, Brazil gives us the impression that this country will continue inventing a new modernism architecture in the future, which is not the recollection of the modern times, but is "current" and advancing the modernism architecture to next level.

一筆書きの建築家である——これは大きな誤解であって，正調なモダニズムを完璧に消化した後にある「達人の技」とも言える様な設計活動なのであり，抽象化された作品の隅々においても空間の正確さは生き続けている。作家性の非常に強い作品を生み出すことで，彼に続く若いジェネレーションの建築家たちに勇気を与えて続けることとなる。それは大スケールの公共建築で見せる自由で壮大な造形のみならず，彼のキャリアにちりばめられた宝石の様な小住宅の名作によっても，因習的な建築様式や言語に縛られることのない，自らの感性を頼りにした独自の建築哲学の可能性を提示している。彼にインスパイアされる若いジェネレーションは，この偉大な巨匠の発散する建築の本質的な力に勇気を得て，彼らの可能性を拡張しているかのように見える。

一方のサン・パウロを本拠地に設計活動をしていたヴィラノヴァ・アルティガスは，建築雑誌などのメディアへの露出をあまり歓迎しない静かなモダニズムの求道者であった。しかし，彼は一連の丹精な作品によって，その後世に多くの若き信者を持つこととなる。打ち放しの荒削りなコンクリートを主に用いて，この国の気質を代弁するかの様な大スケールの力強い空間を創出すると同時に，彼の自邸で見せることになる，内向的，繊細で静かな小空間の住宅建築に至るまで，ブラジルの風土や文化にローカライズしたモダニズム建築を作り上げた。その先見性，良質で普遍的な建築哲学が意外にもブラジル国外には紹介されていないことは残念である。アルティガスはサンパウロ大学で長年教鞭をとり，多くの学生を育成し，その教育者としての功績も大きい。大学において彼のアシスタントをしていたこともあった，次のジェネレーションに位置したのはパウロ・メンデス・ダ・ローシャであった。彼はアルティガスから続く建築哲学を見事に昇華して新しいステージに導き，それをブラジルのみならず世界的に紹介してきたブラジル建築界の功労者である。今号で収録した初期の代表作である彼の自邸において，空間構成，寸法とプロポーション，軽く美しいディテール，光の操作など，彼の建築のエッセンスすべてが既に完成されていることは驚嘆に値する。それらが現在ブラジルで活躍する若手世代に確実に受け継がれ始めていることは，ブラジル建築界のみならず我々にとっても喜ばしいことである。

現代建築のメッカであったアメリカ合衆国は建築においても大量生産の国であった。しかし，1990年頃を境に大きくシフトしていく。ヴァーチャルな空間の出現，社会構造や価値観の変化に伴うアメリカの人々の現代建築に対する興味の喪失，それに伴うアメリカ建築界の後退，失速。この大国に替わって，中南米や，アジア，オーストラリアなど，それまで文化的にも周辺に位置していた国々に大きな芽が出始めてきた。

現在，ブラジルの建築は合衆国や日本で展開されて来たものとは異なる新しいタイプの発展の可能性を秘めていると言えよう。貧困層の問題をはじめ社会的な問題も少なくない国であるが，昨今の経済的な発展，政治の安定化，文化の成熟，そして，世界的なエネルギー・エコロジー問題にいち早く対策をとって来た成果であるバイオエネルギーの推進といったポジティブなファクターがもたらす豊かさは，民族の違いを超えて融合する，新しい社会を作り上げる国民のライフスタイルに貢献するような建築として，モダニズムが依然として有効であるという手応えがある。

現在，この国は，近代を顧みるような懐古趣味ではない，「今」を進行しているモダニズム建築を今後生み出して行く予感を我々に与えている。

Itamambuca Beach, Brazil

巨匠の住宅 — Residential Masterpieces
Architect's House   Paulo Mendes da Rocha
São Paulo, SP, Brazil 1960
Photos by Y. Futagawa

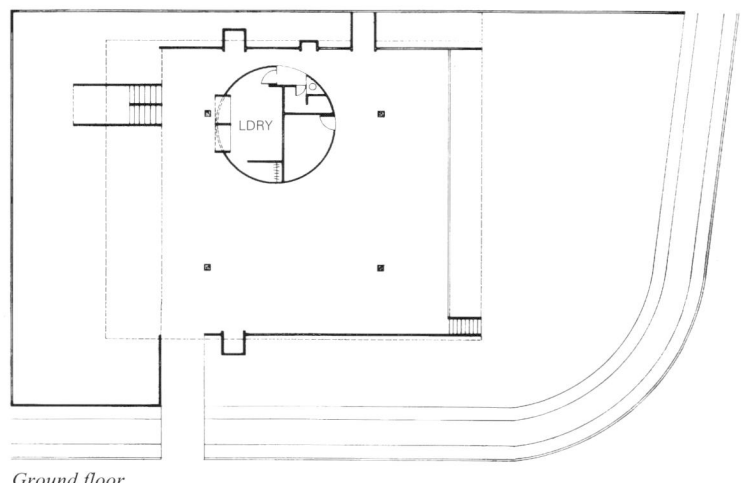

Ground floor

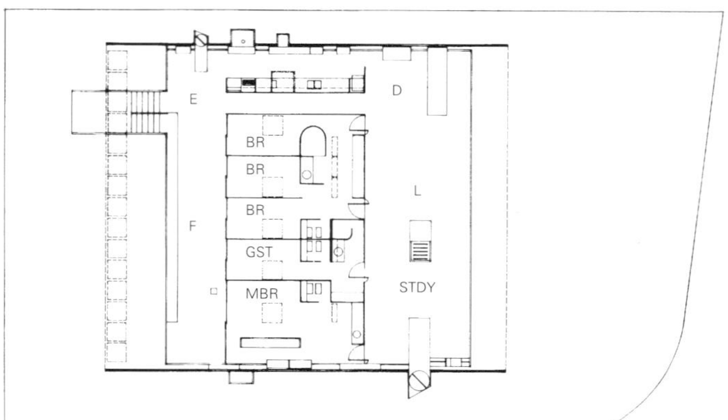

First floor (original version of 1960, partitions between bedrooms are changed later)

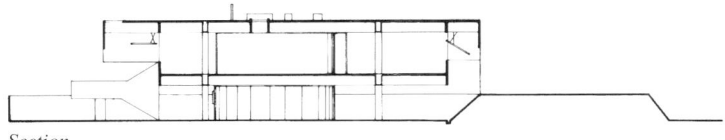
View from street 道路側全景

Section

Corner detail　角部ディテール

Approach　アプローチ

Wall detail with aperture　壁に取り付けられた採光用の窓

Approach アプローチ

Laundry room ランドリー・ルーム

Approach: staircase to entrance on right　アプローチ：右は玄関へ至る階段

Approach: laundry room on right　アプローチ：右はランドリー・ルーム

Entrance 玄関

Pilotis ピロティ

View from entrance: living room at the end of corridor 玄関より見る：廊下の先は居間

△▽*Family room*　ファミリー・ルーム

Opening of living room 居間の開口部

Living room originally used as bedroom　居間。以前は寝室として使われていた

It is located within a quiet residential area in the suburb of São Paulo. Although around 50 years have passed since its construction, and its outline of the building is now hidden by the surrounding grown up trees, the bold presence of this house has not decreased or changed yet.

A volume in the length and width of 15 m, along with the height of one floor level, is lifted up by 4 columns and a circular core volume (a laundry space). The embankment in 2 m high is placed at the boundary of the site and the road, and it surrounds the pilotis space. This acts as a buffers to properly cut off the visibility from the surrounding, and provide a functionality as a foyer space to the house. A thin concrete beam projected out from the inside also works as the eaves to cast an atmospheric shade over the entrance approach.

The interior space in one floor consists of a living space and a family room on both edges of the volume, while the bedrooms are sandwiched between them. The walls dividing each room are about 3 cm, thin concrete wall, and they do not function as structures. In other words, the building was designed from the beginning to adapt and transform, according to the shifting of a lifestyle of the resident. Actually, the room designated as the main bedroom at the completion of the building is now used as a corridor space to circulate around the interior space; also the bedrooms have been transformed into a living space or to a study space.

Only the living space and the family room open up with transparent faces, with still beautiful flap windows bordered by thin steel frames. The simple but subtle detail adapting to the climate of Brazil, is in harmony with the massiveness of the concrete... no, actually with the placement of rather thin board walls. The concrete slab enclosed by a "U-shaped" wall have top lights and small openings to cast atmospheric rays of light into the dimly lit interior spaces. In addition, all the fixtures ranging from the dining table, the fireplace, the shelves, to the shower room—are all produced in concrete, which was intended to extend the possibility of the usage of concrete.

Paulo Mendes da Rocha taught at university for a long period of time—therefore today, almost all young architects who play active part of the architecture field in today's Brazil are the "children" of Mendes da Rocha, and the root of his strong influence can be found within this housing project. How a little operation and a simple structure system—that is to say, the building produced by lifting up a concrete, rectangular volume by a piloti system—can achieve a diversity of a building? The spirit of Modernism to seek for the answer to such question is taken over by the architects in today's Brazil.

◁△*Bedrooms transformed into study (left) and living room (right)*
寝室は，現在，書斎（左）や居間（右）として使われている

　サンパウロ郊外の閑静な住宅地。完成してから約50年を経たこの住宅は，生い茂る樹木に建物の輪郭を覆われながらも，その強い存在感に変わりはない。
　約15メートル角，一層分のヴォリュームが，4本の柱と丸いコア（ランドリー・スペース）で持ち上げられている。道路との境界に盛土された高さ2メートルほどの堤がピロティを囲み，適度に視線を遮ることで，家全体のホワイエとして機能している。エントランス・アプローチの上部には，内部から伸びた薄いコンクリートの梁が庇となって印象的な影を落とす。
　内部は，ワンフロアの両端に置かれた居間とファミリー・ルームに挟まれるようにして，寝室が並ぶ。それらを仕切る壁は3センチ程の薄いコンクリート造で，これは構造壁ではない。つまり，住まい方の変化に様々に対応できるように当初から意図されていた。実際，完成当時，主寝室だった場所は，全体を回遊できるよう廊下となり，寝室も居間や書斎へと姿を変えてきた。
　コの字型に覆われたコンクリート・スラブの所々に穿たれたトップライトや壁の小さな開口部から，ほの暗い室内に印象的な光が差し込む。両側の居間とファミリールームのみが全面開口部に接し，細いスティールで縁取られた跳ね上げ式の窓は今でも美しい。ブラジルの気候に合わせた簡素で繊細なそのディテールは，コンクリートのマッシブな，という

よりは，薄い板壁のような設えと調和を成している。また，ダイニング・テーブルや暖炉，本棚，シャワー・ルームに至るまで，建具はすべてコンクリート製だということも大きな特徴である。コンクリートの思いがけない汎用性の高さに気づかされる。
　メンデス・ダ・ローシャは，長く大学の教鞭に立ち，今，ブラジルで活躍する若手建築家のほとんどが，彼の「子供たち」である。その大きな影響力の源をこの家に見ることができるだろう。すなわち，コンクリートの矩形のヴォリュームをピロティで持ち上げ，いかに少ない操作とシンプルな構造で，そこに多様性を獲得するか。そのモダニズムの精神は，ブラジルの今に受け継がれている。

Corridor between bedrooms: partition and desk are made of concrete
寝室の間の廊下：パーティション，机はコンクリート製

Shower room made of concrete
コンクリート製のシャワー・ルーム

Corridor with natural light through small aperture: used as master bedroom originally　所々穿たれた小さな開口部から自然光の入る廊下：元は主寝室として使われていた

Living room 居間

△▽▷ *Living room: fireplace and bookshelves are made of concrete*　居間：コンクリート製の暖炉と本棚が置かれる

Study beside living room 居間脇の書斎

Study　書斎

Corridor: view toward entrance　廊下：正面先は玄関

Dining table made of concrete　コンクリート製のダイニング・テーブル

Bathroom　浴室

Kitchen　台所

△▷ *Entrance* 玄関

A dialogue with editor

Angelo Bucci
アンジェロ・ブッチ

Interview: Yoshio Futagawa　聞き手：二川由夫

Angelo Bucci: The House in Aldeia da Serra (GAH105) was designed in 2001 at MMBB Arquitetos, my former office. I remember when José Henrique and Beatriz as the owners asked me to design their house, in our first meeting they brought some books show me their preferences. I got really impressive, because their books were about the work of the best architects. It was not by chance they were so sharp talking about their house project during the process, it was always a great conversation.

My former office were composed by Fernando de Mello Franco, Marta Moreira, Milton Braga and myself. Milton was a very important interlocutor in this project, also Ibsen Puleo Uvo the structure engineer. Actually it is an advantage to have the possibility of working with them.

GA: Did you all go together to the same school in São Paulo University?

Bucci: Yes, all of us met each other by the first time there, at the School of Architecture of the University of São Paulo, FAUUSP, inside that gorgeous building designed by Vilanova Artigas. That school offered me the most important thing: a group of people whose interest about architecture made us good friends and allowed us to discover a way to become an architect in Brazil. Alvaro Puntoni and Alvaro Razuk, who were my partners in my first office, were also very important in my background. Even nowadays, when I am teaching at that same school, it is still offering me some new interlocutors like Marcos Acayaba, Alexandre Delijaicov and Antonio Carlos Barossi.

Of course the school offers also all that institutionalized knowledge: great masters and masterpieces. But, what I am saying is that our peers are who provide life to everything.

GA: One of the main topics that I wanted to talk about is your background, because Brazil is a really rare country where the modernist concept is preserved, not interrupted like it was in the US or Europe by new movements such as post-modernism or constructivism. Now they are finally trying to move back to modernism but in Brazil I think that somehow the idea is preserved and developed in like way and finally getting here now.

Figures like Lucio Costa, Oscar Neimeyer, Vilancva Arigas or even Paulo Mendes da Rocha may be your source of influence, so maybe you can analyze not only yourself but the general situation of the Brazilian architecture as a mecca of modernism.

Bucci: A mecca of modernism.... it is an interesting approach.

If I think about my background I think first of all about my birthplace. Orlandia is the name of my town, a 20,000 people place or exactly one thousand times smaller than São Paulo city. I lived there until my eighteen. It was also there the place where I could design my first projects as soon as I had finished the School of Architecture. Then, I was designing some small buildings to be built far away from where I was living [São Paulo is 400 km far from Orlandia], in such way that I could not visit the construction site as often as I would like to do. I learned to believe in drawings as the only way I had to communicate what would like to build. A lot of my background comes from my childhood, my

アンジェロ・ブッチ 「アルデイア・ダ・セラの家」(GAH105)は以前の事務所，MMBBアルキテートスで2001年に設計したものです。クライアントであるジョゼ・ヘンリックとベアトリズに自宅の設計を依頼された時，彼らは参考にと，建築関係の本を何冊か最初の打ち合わせに持って来てくれたのですが，その意識の高さにかなり驚いた記憶があります。プロジェクトについての話し合いを重ねる間にも当然，的を得た鋭い意見が出て来ていました。

当時の事務所に所属していたのは，フェルナンド・メロ・フランコ，マルタ・モレイラ，ミウトン・ブラガと私です。ミウトンは，構造担当のイブセン・プエオ・ウヴォと共に，このプロジェクトにおける重要なパートナーでした。彼らと一緒に仕事をできたのは大きな強みだといえます。

GA 皆さんはサン・パウロ大学の同じ学部で学ばれたのですか？

ブッチ ええ。全員，「サン・パウロ大学建築・都市計画学部」（FAUUSP）で出会いました。あのヴィラノヴァ・アルティガス設計の素晴らしい校舎で。学校で得た最も大切なものは，彼らとの出会いです。建築への志を通じて友情を育み，各々がブラジルで建築家として進むべき道を模索しました。最初の事務所で一緒だったアルヴァロ・プントーニとアルヴァロ・ラズークも私の人生の中で重要な人物です。母校で教鞭をとるようになった今でも，あそこではマルコス・アカヤバ，アレクサンドル・デリジャイコブや，アントニオ・カルロス・バロッシといった人々との新たな出会いがありました。

もちろん，偉大な建築家や名作などについて学問的な知識を得た場所でもありますが，やはりあの頃に出会った仲間たちが今の私を作ったといえます。

GA お聞きしたいことの一つに，あなたのバックグラウンドがあります。ブラジルはモダニズムのコンセプトが保たれている，非常に稀有な国です。欧米のように，ポスト・モダンや構成主義といった新しいムーブメントによる断絶がみられない。欧米は今になって結局モダニズムへと戻ろうとしているわけですが，ブラジルでは何とかそれが保たれ，そして進化を遂げていると思うのです。

ルシオ・コスタ，オスカー・ニーマイヤー，ヴィラノヴァ・アルティガス，パウロ・メンデス・ダ・ローシャといった先達があなたに影響を与えているのでしょうから，モダニズムのメッカとしてのブラジル建築の現状についてもお話していただきたいのですが。

ブッチ モダニズムのメッカですか……，面白い見方ですね。

自分の経歴を振り返ってみて，まず一番大切なのは生まれた場所だと思います。生まれ故郷はオランディアという街で，人口2万人ですからサン・パウロのちょうど1000分の1の大きさです。18歳までそこで暮らしました。大学を卒業してから最初に手掛けた設計もそこでの仕事でした。その後，自分の住む街から遠く離れた場所に計画される小規模な建物を設計するようになって（サン・パウロはオランディアから400キロ離れている），思うように建築現場を訪れることができなくなりました。自分が何を作りたいかを伝える唯一の手段はドローイングなのだと強く思うようにもなりました。自分では，幼年期や家族，故郷の街から大いに影響を受けていると思います。

サン・パウロはとても魅力的な場所です。最初に

family and my town.

São Paulo is a stunning experience. Since 1983, when I came here by the very first time in order to begin the Architecture School, I have learned a lot by living in this city. That first shock I had was just the beginning of a long learning process from two most important "actors" or sources: the city of São Paulo and the Architecture School Building designed by Vilanova Artigas.

São Paulo is potentially everything I can learn. You think about Brazil as a mecca of modernism, of course, modern was our first possibility. Maybe it is our only one. It is a sort of our only architecture. Even the history or everything that came before is modern as well here in Brazil. The people who showed us our past, they are also and at the same time our modern architects.

Lucio Costa, for instance, he "created" the Brazilian colonial architecture because he revealed us that period as a way to provide us one specific and chosen starting point. It was also him the author of the plan to Brasília. In the thirties when he invited Le Corbusier to be the principal of the MEC design team, Lucio Costa was deciding who would be our modern precedent.

I would like to highlight that to be able to choose who will be your precedent is a quite modern attitude.

I agree with you that it is possible to recognize here a tradition of modern architecture. It is remarkable in the works of some great masters like Vilanova Artigas, Paulo Mendes da Rocha and Lina Bo Bardi. But it is clear that we had here an attempted interruption of this process. The whole seventies was a very hard time. Then we were under the dictatorship, since 69 Vilanova Artigas and Paulo Mendes da Rocha had been expelled from the University. It is quite symptomatic that it is so hard to find nowadays an architect that had attended the university in that time working with design buildings nowadays. There is just a very small and remarkable group, I can name them: Francisco Fanucci, Marcelo Ferraz, Marcelo Suzuki, Andre Vainer, Guilherme Paoliello. They became architects also because they could find a kind of refuge working with Lina Bo Bardi during that time. The next decade, the eighties, was not so different. It means twenty years of a violent interruption.

Anyway, it is true that here in Brazil some ideas or concepts were preserved, or resisted. How they could overcome twenty years? I think that the building designed by Vilanova Artigas played a important role in this resistance, it is like if the building had kept talking some lessons while people could not speak. Also, Lina Bo Bardi played a role by offering a refuge to that young group of architects. Paulo Mendes da Rocha played an incredible role by overcoming himself through those years and by being able to talk with the whole world nowadays. The resistance was also possible due to thousands of other people. Including those architects that, after a twenty years break and without any link with the precedent generation, when they found themselves in a modern condition because they had to "choose their precedents" they decided that the Brazilian modern architecture

Fig.1. V. Artigas: Faculty of Architecture and Urban Planning, University of São Paulo (FAUUSP) Thousands of students gathered in the central atrium of University
Fig.1. V・アルティガス：サン・パウロ大学建築・都市計画学部。大勢の学生が中央のアトリウムに集まる様子

Fig.2. Anhangabaú, downton of São Paulo Millions of people claim for their right to vote for president
Fig.2. サン・パウロ中心部，アニャンガバウ。大勢の人々が大統領選の選挙権を主張して集まる様子

spbr arquitetos: House in Ubatuba Beach, 2005- (under construction)

ここに来たのは1983年，大学入学のため。ここでの生活ではたくさんのことを学びました。初めて受けた衝撃は，それに続く長い学習過程の始まりに過ぎなかった。その立役者というか源となったのが，サン・パウロ市と，ヴィラノヴァ・アルティガスによる建築学部の校舎です。

サン・パウロは私が学ぼうとしたもの全てを内包していました。さっきブラジルはモダニズムのメッカ，とおっしゃいましたね。勿論，モダンは我々の最初の選択肢でした。唯一の，だったかもしれない。ここには現代の建築しかないのかもしれない。歴史や，それ以前にあったすべてのものまでが，ブラジルではモダンだったのです。我々に過去について教えてくれた人々もまた，現代の建築家たちでしたから。

例えば，ルシオ・コスタ。彼はブラジルの植民地建築を「創った」のです。あの時代を一つの始発点として選び出し，我々に提示してくれた。また，彼はブラジリアのプランの作者でもあります。30年代にル・コルビュジエを「教育保健省」の設計チームのリーダーに招いたとき，ルシオ・コスタは，誰をモダニズムの先駆者とするのか決定を下したのです。

そして，自分たちの前例となる人を自らの手で選択できる，というのは極めて現代的な姿勢だ，と思います。

あなたがおっしゃるように，ここには現代建築の「伝統」がある。ヴィラノヴァ・アルティガス，パウロ・メンデス・ダ・ローシャやリナ・ボー・バルディといった偉大な建築家たちの作品を見ればわかります。しかし，その過程には大きな断絶があった。70年代は大変に困難な10年間でした。独裁政権下の69年，ヴィラノヴァ・アルティガスとパウロ・メンデス・ダ・ローシャは大学から追放されました。当時の大学に在籍して，今日も設計を続けている建築家というのは数が極端に少なく，フランシスコ・ファヌッシ，マルセロ・フェラーズ，マルセロ・スズキ，アンドレ・ヴァイナー，ギエーム・パオリエーロといった面々くらいしかいません。彼らは当時リナ・ボー・バルディと仕事をすることで一種の避難をすることができたから建築家になれたのです。その次の世代，80年代も似たようなものでした。つまり20年間もの凄まじい断絶があるのです。

確かにブラジルでは，ある種のアイディアやコンセプトが「維持」され，あるいは生き延びている，と言えます。あの20年間をどうやってやり過ごしたのでしょう？　私が思うに，ヴィラノヴァ・アルティガスの建物がそのレジスタンスの中で重要な役割を果たしたのではないでしょうか。人々が言論を封じられていた間も，建物がずっと語り続けていた，と。また，リナ・ボー・バルディが若い建築家たちに避難場所を与えたという功績もあります。パウロ・メンデス・ダ・ローシャはあの時代を自力で乗り越え，今なお世界を相手に活躍できているという意味で途方もない役割を果たしています。他にも多くの人々がこのレジスタンスを担ってきました。その中には，20年の空白の後，前の世代と何のつながりも持たないまま，現代的な状況に置かれたとき，つまり「自らの先駆者の選択」を迫られたときに，ブラジルの現代建築を出発点にしようと決定した建築家たちもいました。これは維持というよりもレジスタンスに近い姿勢です。

そして，我々はヴィラノヴァ・アルティガスが「FAUUSP」の校舎に残した言葉から学びました。

would be their starting point. It is more resistance than preservation.

If we learned from those masters it was possible as a result of that resistance. We learn Vilanova Artigas from the words lingered on the building he designed for FAUUSP. I could say that building designed by him is everything I can learn, exactly as I said about the city of São Paulo. Of course this is almost a Vilanova Artigas quotation: the city like the house, the house like the city. [Fig.1, 2] What is remarkable in these words is the idea of "fragment", like small pieces of a whole. I think this idea is important in the work of the most important architects in São Paulo. If you take the Baeta House designed by Vilanova Artigas in 57, that structure could be understood as exaggerated, but it is the opposite if you take the whole house as just a small piece of something much bigger. The house does not finish at the door step, according to his own words.

It is a similar speech if you take the Chapel in Campos do Jordao designed by Paulo Mendes da Rocha. There is just one huge column like if the Chapel was just a fragment extract from a gothic cathedral. For an architect this reasoning is a powerful way of think about the city as a collection of fragments and each one of them as a source for new arrangements. The FGV School designed by Paulo Mendes da Rocha in 94 is described by himself as having its matrix [spatial disposition] apprehended from Viaduto do Chá and its surrounding buildings.

Although the notion of environment was not present there, it is possible, by following this reasoning, to take the city as an environment. I mean a whole without contour lines, a whole that can just be embraced by its fragments.

GA: But you may find how important it is that problem after you go to other countries. People may make you realize how the difference between your country and the others in other parts of the world is so noisy. Too many resources and too much information will not produce a concept or product in pure form. I think that is why people now focus on the architecture and culture here.

Rem Koolhaas mentioned that modernism growing in tropical, warm condition is the right way. Here, Australian, or Asian countries. In colder countries people make concepts and ideologies.

Bucci: It grows in warm conditions like trees? I don't think so

You said too many resources... I think that "lots of resources and lack of meaning" is a challenge for architects nowadays. Which is the line between both resources and meanings? It is all those lines that apart the world by geographical positions, weather conditions, economical situation, cultures, races etc. One owns the resources but doesn't know the demands. One is able to do but can't understand why. This is a not acceptable situation. I don't believe that architecture concepts and actions, or theory and practice, can be separated. Architecture is a judgment through an action, is a theory through a practice. The whole world means [when taken by its fragments] the totality of our possibilities. An architectonic proposal is an action and an action is a no doubt event. There is no a misunderstood architect because to be understood is a

spbr arquitetos: House in Ubatuba Beach

Studio: blackboard to discuss idea promptly
スタジオ：アイディアはすぐに黒板で検討する

precondition to one becomes an architect. It is exactly in the same way there is no an inexistent architecture.

Maybe the distance between theory and practice [also project and construction] has produced a sort of weak imagination. I mean a kind of illusion where one imagines a project without realizing exactly how it will be built, like if it were a shortcut between a rough first idea and the final result of a long and chained process of its development. But there is no shortcut. I think about construction as a clear aim for architects tasks, as a way to keep our imagination process strong and enable to succeed.

When we talk among our peers architects, we are always talking about our everyday tasks. We are talking about those simple questions we have to deal or what we have to solve in order to design. These everyday tasks are very similar in any place, they are always very simple questions [the meaning of what we design is not so easy, the images we work during the imagination process is not a simple question]. I enjoy this conversation or the possibility to exchange experiences among my peers because it makes me consider about the validity or reasons of doing what we are doing. This consideration decreases the proportion of issues we do automatically during the designing process.

I mean, instead of just inherit or assume some ready solutions, during a designing process we can check as much as we can if a solution is or not the case to be adopted. Because a solution makes sense in a specific context, if it succeed we tends to assume it automatically, like if it was by assumption always a positive thing. But context is changing all the time.

In the Brazilian context, you can take an example like a double layer-glass window. Here, with all the social prejudice it means high standard, sign of status, but it absolutely doesn't make sense in a place like Bahia where you can sleep on the beach every night having the whole sky as a ceiling, without warm clothes and we all know that it will be very comfortable. Why do we have to use a double-layer glass if any glass is necessary at all? We don't even have to insulate the inside and the outside. We should allow the air goes through the window.

You visited our architecture school, FAU-USP, and you could see that it is a doorless building. It sound simple to describe, it is a building without doors, but it is not so easy to be able to design it properly, because you have to be able to imagine it before, you have to consider that it will be a doorless building previously to start the design process. I mean you have to be free of a lot of things you learned very well. Vilanova Artigas knew how to design that building without doors Such way to think about architecture, as a method, is also very powerful. It is that same modern condition: we are able to choose what we will or not inherit. It is like if we were not the result of our past, but our past is also a choice from the present. This reasoning after centuries of colonialism is really powerful.

GA: How was the House in Rio de Janeiro (GAH106)? Please let me know the strategy for this project.

Bucci: Paulo and Rosa, the owners, when they came here to talk with me by the first time they

Angelo Bucci (MMBB arquitetos): Casa em Aldeia da Serra, 2001-02

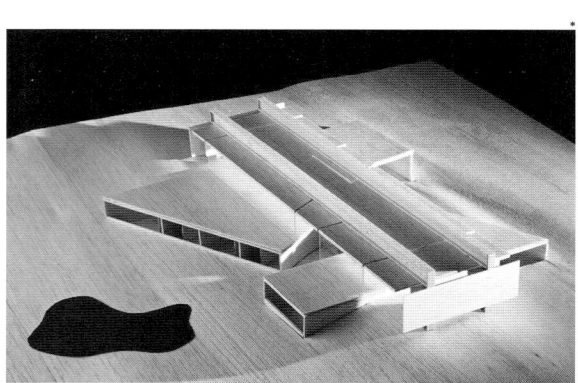

spbr arquitetos: House in East Hampton, 2007-

brought me this picture showing an amazing view of the Sugarloaf and Guanabara Bay and they told me: you bought this place to build our house. I think they were right, the view was more important than the site itself. But it was not so simple to enjoy that view. They explained me that to be able to shot that picture they had walk up to the first plateau 20 m higher than the street level. It was not enough. Then, they reached the second plateau 5 m higher on the very top. It was not enough yet. Finally they climb a tree to look toward the south and just then they could see that amazing view. I like to say that the idea of this project is not mine, it came from that tree. It's a joke that I like to say that a project is not just an idea, it results of a long chained designing process.

If you look at the section of the House in Rio de Janeiro you realize that it is a kind of exploded building: bedrooms as a long block over the first plateau, living room over the second plateau having that beautiful view as a permanent picture and a void space in between both, like if the open space could be enclosed to became one level of this building. Swimming pool area and kitchen were placed in this open level. Around one year after I had designed this house I went to visit Paulo in his birth place, a small house in the countryside of Minas Gerais. It was a great surprise when I realized that there, in the house where Paulo had been born the kitchen was outside. This kind of arrangement used to be the mainstream in that place, because if we think about our demands free from architectonic prejudice, then it is easy to realize that is better to avoid heating the whole house with a wood stove. Maybe this house in Rio de Janeiro is just as modern as that small house where he was born.

June 9th, 2008, at studio of spbr arquitetos

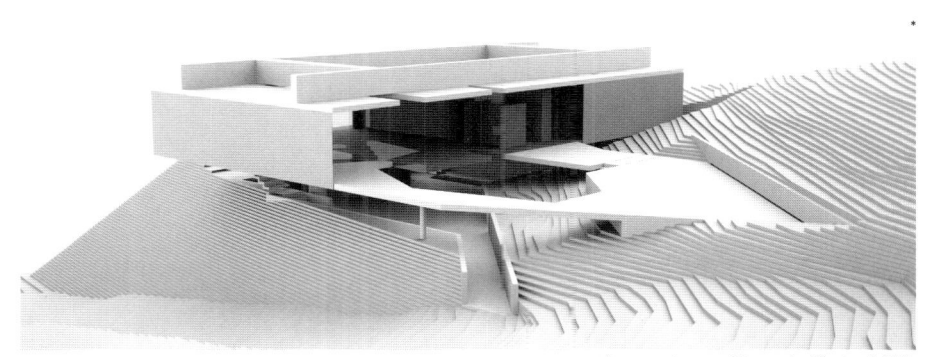

spbr arquitetos: House in Cotia, 2008-

photos except as noted: GA photographers
* photos provided by spbr arquitetos
** photo by Mario Dallari Bucci

SPBR ARQUITETOS

HOUSE IN RIO DE JANEIRO

Rio de Janeiro, RJ, Brazil
Design: 2004 Construction: 2005–08

Photos: Y. Futagawa

Overall view from northeast: living room wing (left) and bedroom wing (right)　北東側全景：居間棟（左）と寝室棟（右）

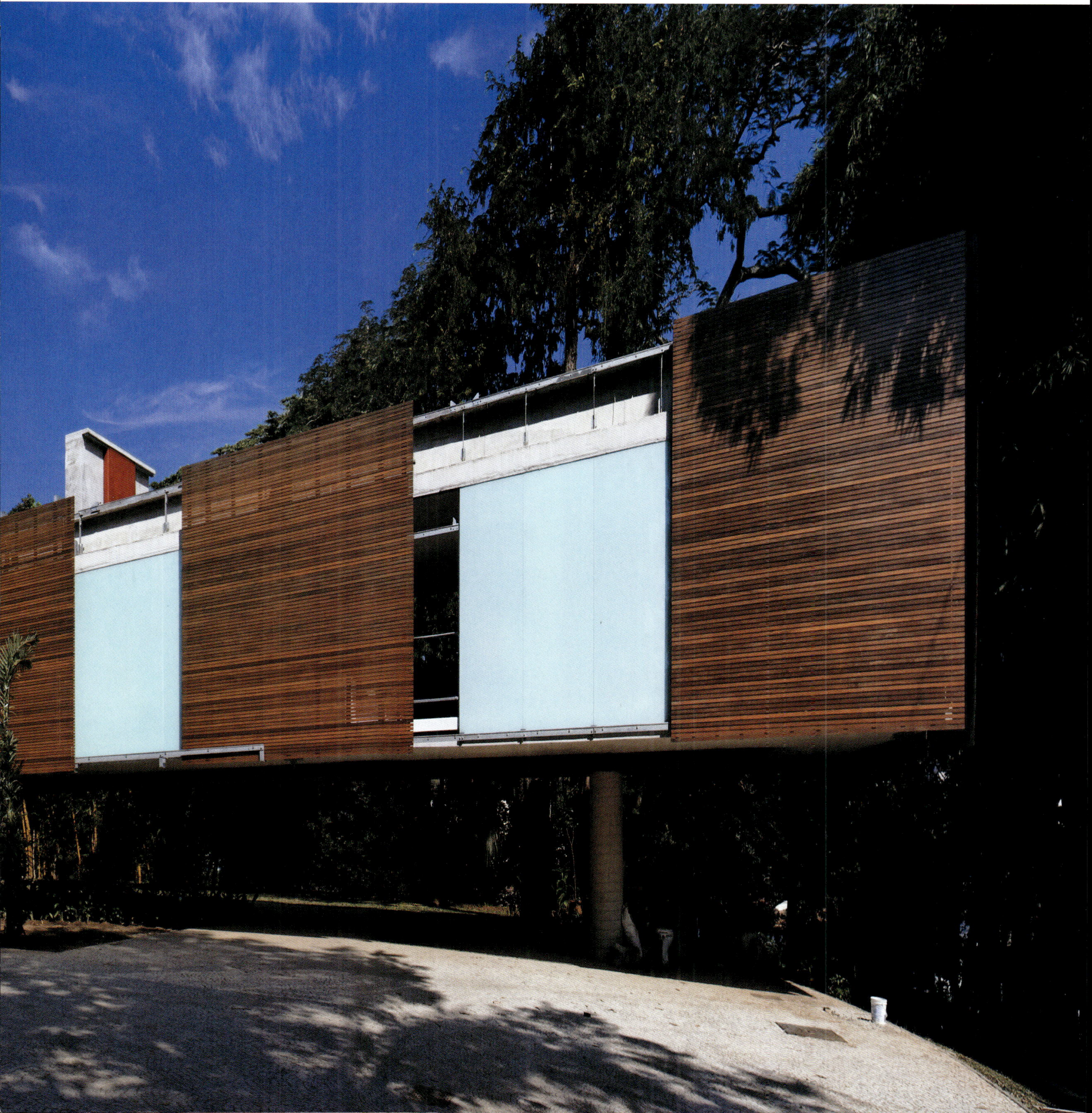

Santa Teresa is a historical neighborhood that offers some great views of the city of Rio de Janeiro. The house is located in one of the highest points of Santa Teresa's hill. From the north side of the house it is possible to see the old downtown; from the south side, a more panoramic view of Pão de Açucar and the Guanabara Bay. The site starts at 100 m above sea level at the cable car street and finishes at 125 m at a breathtaking viewpoint of Pão de Açucar.

The project takes into consideration the two pre-existent levels of the pronounced topography: 120 m and 125 m over sea level. At the lower level, there is a linear block that leads to the bedrooms and the studio. Their main glass facade opens up to the enjoying garden on the east side. These two prismatic and linear volumes are opened on the east and west sides but are completely closed on the north and south sides, leaving the ground under them empty. The roof was designed to make a complementary ground on the upper plateau.

The living room is located over the higher plateau providing a view of downtown on the north side and of the Guanabara Bay and Pão de Açucar on the south. This volume is closed on the east and west sides to avoid sun heat and to emphasize the magnificent views on the other sides. It leaves the level below completely open. Thus, there is a bare level between bedrooms and living room which is filled by the kitchen, where, according to the traditional Brazilian culture, most people will spend their spare time. It is a spread out and blown-up construction that should become part of Rio de Janeiro's landscape.

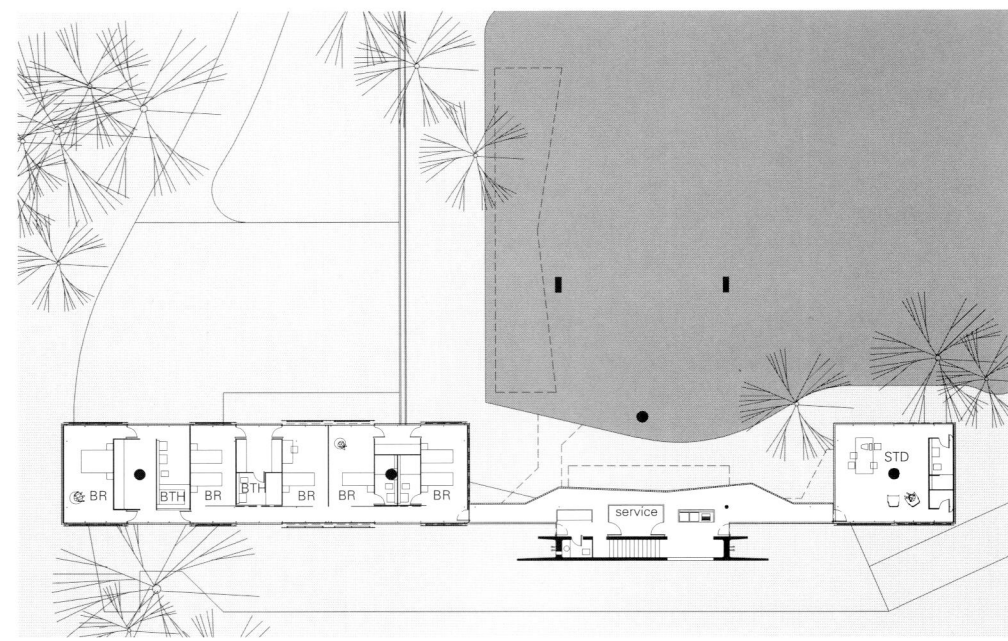

Level 122.5 m

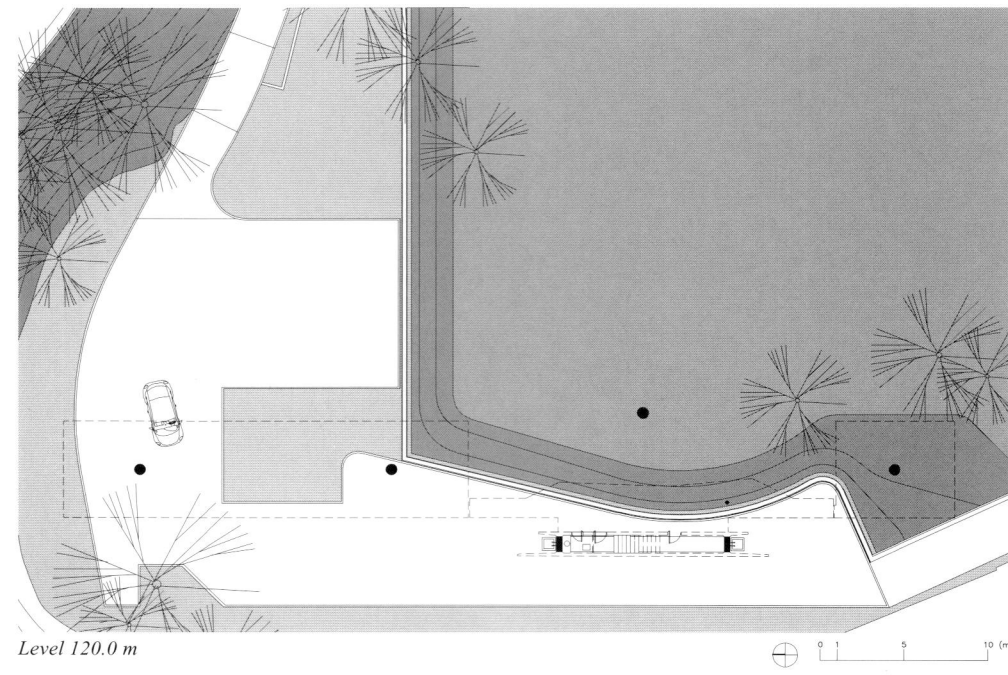

Level 120.0 m

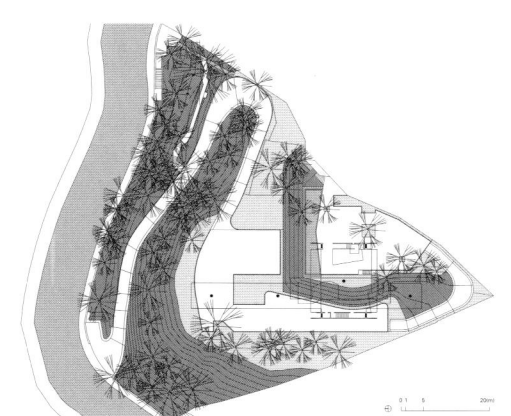

Site plan

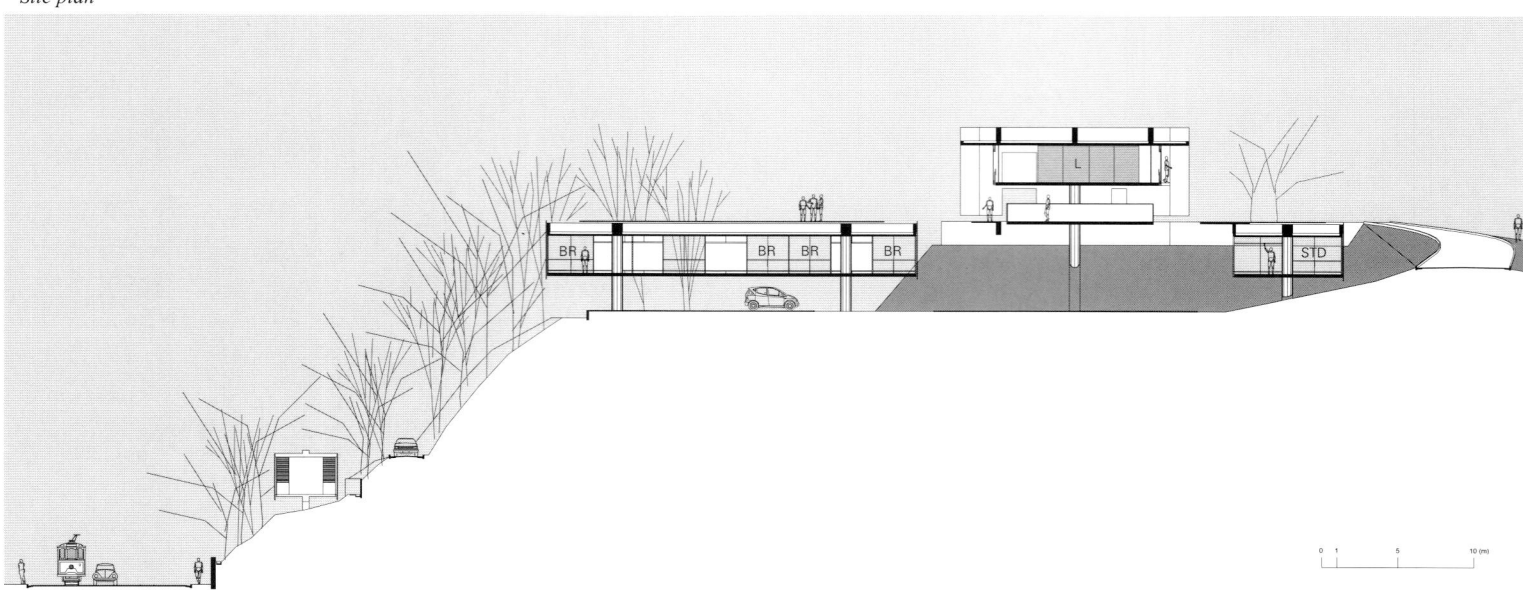

Longitudinal section 1

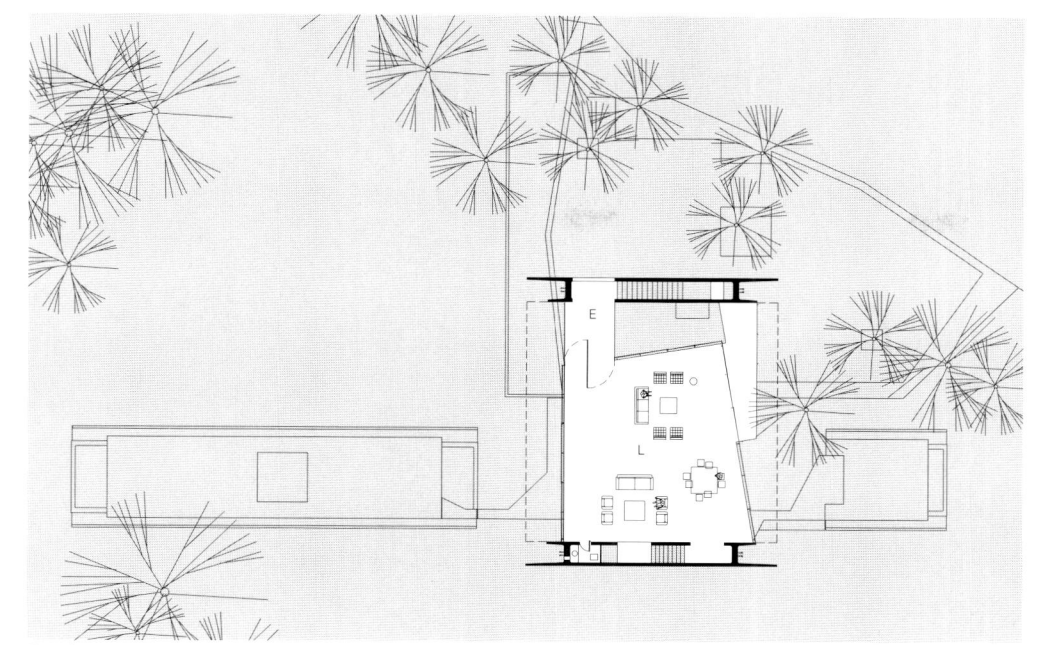

Level 128.6 m

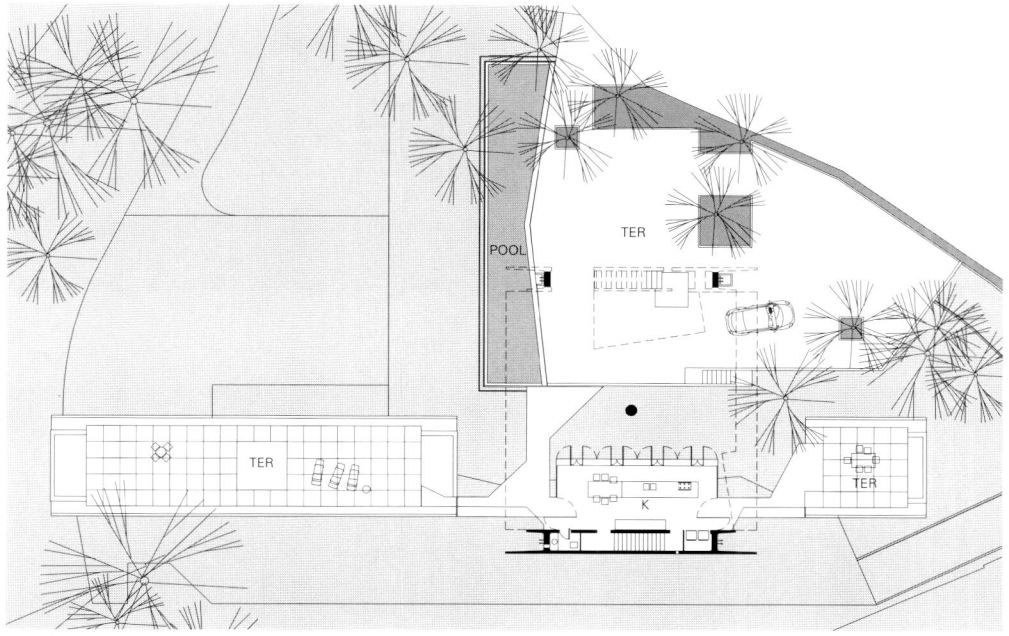

Level 126.0 m

サンタ・テレサは，リオ・デ・ジャネイロの素晴らしい眺望が得られる歴史的な郊外地区である。この住宅は，サンタ・テレサの丘で最も高い部分の一つに位置している。北側からは，旧市街中心部を眺めることができ，南側からはより広々としたパン・デ・アレカス山とグアナバラ湾を眺めることができる。敷地は，海抜100メートル地点のケーブルカーが走る道路から始まり，海抜125メートルの息をのむほど素晴らしい眺めの地点で終わっている。

ここでは，海抜120メートル及び125メートルという，敷地が元々持つ2つの明快な地形レベルを考慮している。

低い方のレベルには寝室とスタジオに通じる直線的なブロックがある。寝室とスタジオのガラスのファサードに，東側の楽しい庭に向かって開いている。この二つのプリズムのような直線的なヴォリュームは，東側と西側に向けて開いているが，北側と南側には完全に閉じており，下部の地盤は空隙にしてある。屋根は，上層の台地を補完するようにデザインされている。

リビングルームは，上層の台地の上に位置して，北側では中心市街地の眺めが得られ，南側ではグアナバラ湾とパン・デ・アルカス山の眺めが得られる。このヴォリュームは，東側と西側を閉じて太陽熱を避けつつ，北側と南側の雄大な眺めを際立たせている。このレベルの下部は，完全にオープンにしてある。従って，寝室とリビングルームのレベルの間には余白があり，そこに台所を設けた。ブラジルの伝統的な文化では，大半の人は台所で余暇を過ごす。

この作品は，リオ・デ・ジャネイロの景観の一部となるように広がり，膨らんでいく建築である。

Architects: spbr arquitetos—Angelo Bucci, principal-in-charge; Ciro Miguel, Juliana Braga, Suzana Jeque, project team
Clients: Paulo Lopes, Rosa Bertholdo
Consultants: Jorge Zaven Kurkdjian, structural; Fernando Magalhães Chacel, landscape
Structural system: reinforced concrete
Major materials: concrete, glass
Site area: 4,483.65 m²
Total floor area: 481.41 m²
Costs: US$ 800,000.00

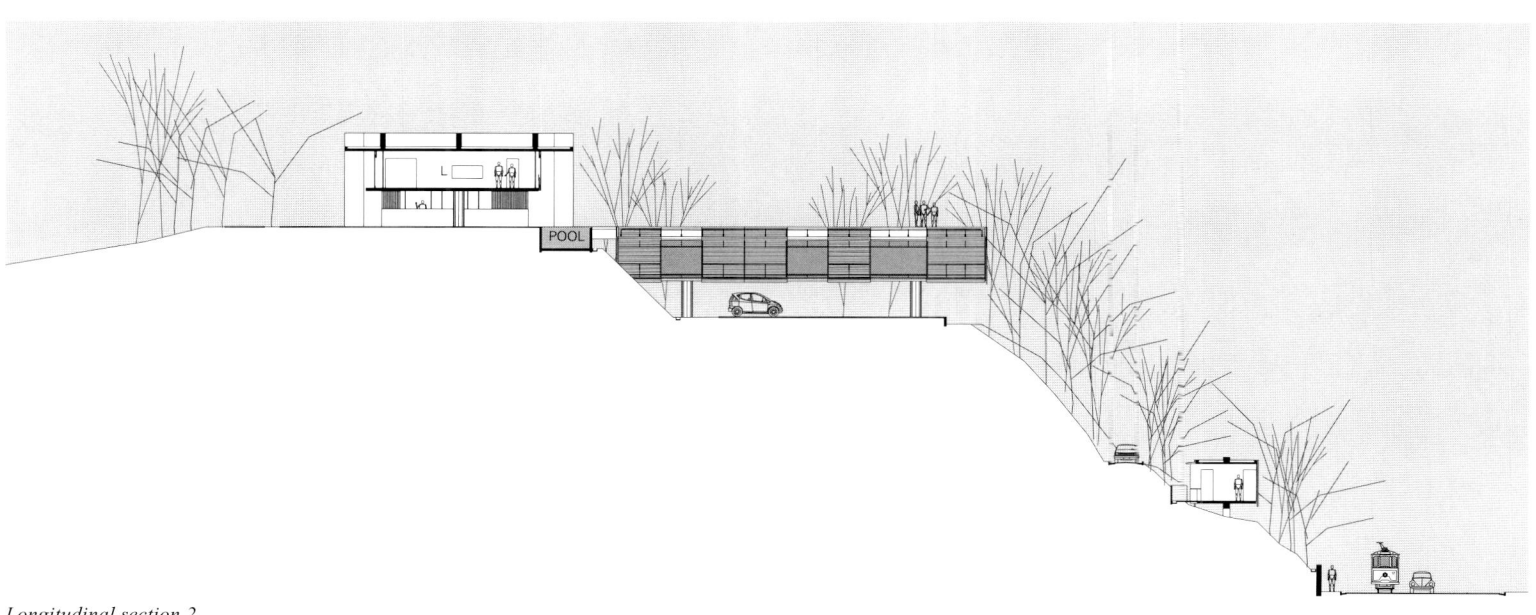

Longitudinal section 2

Bedroom wing on north 北側，寝室棟

Bedroom wing: pilotis 寝室棟：ピロティ

View toward living room wing: bedroom wing on right　居間棟を見る：右は寝室棟

Terrace of living room wing　居間棟のテラス

45

Living room wing (left) and bedroom wing (right)　居間棟（左）と寝室棟（右）

Living room wing. terrace with pool　居間棟：プールのあるテラス

View toward living room wing from roof terrace of bedroom wing 寝室棟の屋上より居間棟を見る

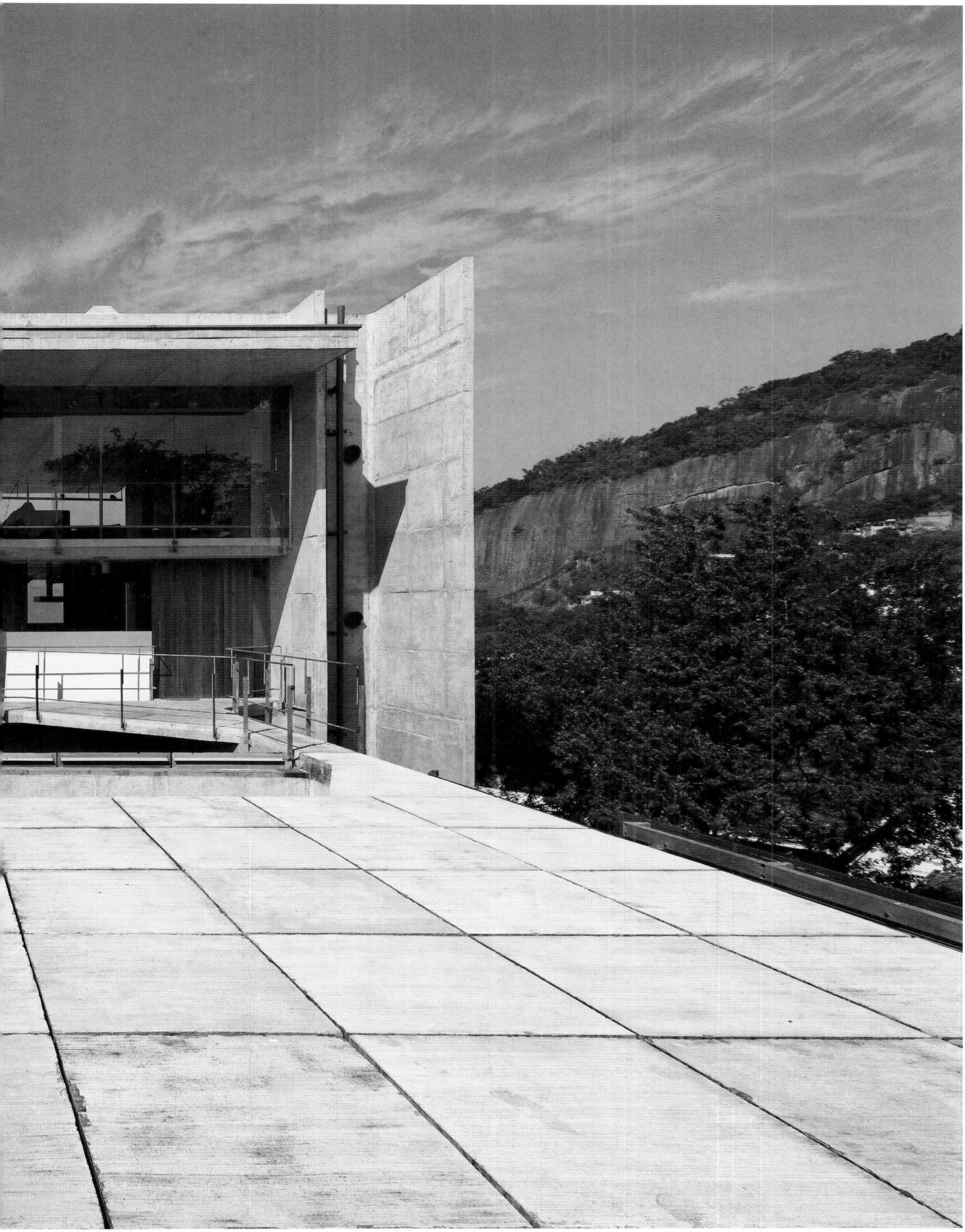

View toward north from terrace of living room wing　居間棟のテラスより北を見る

Void between terrace (left) and kichen (right): view toward studio　テラス（左）と台所（右）の間のヴォイド：スタジオを見る

View toward kitchen from terrace over void　テラスよりヴォイド越しに台所を見る

Kitchen　台所

Living room on top floor: looking south　最上階にある居間：南を見る

53

View toward living room wing from south　南より居間棟を見る

View from south end of terrace: living room on upper floor (right)　テラス南端部より見る：上階は居間（右）

Void on sloping ground　傾斜した庭上のヴォイド

△▽*View from top floor*　最上階からの眺め

Kitchen: looking south 台所：南を見る

Corridor between bedroom wing and studio　寝室棟とスタジオを繋ぐ廊下

Corridor of bedroom wing　寝室棟の廊下

△▷ *Corridor along bedrooms*　寝室脇の廊下

△▷ *Bedroom*　寝室

59

SPBR ARQUITETOS

HOUSE IN CARAPICUIBA

São Paulo, SP, Brazil
Design: 2003 Construction: 2004–08

Photos: Yoshio F.

Geographic Conditions
The most remarkable feature of the site where the house is located is its depression, in topographical terms. From the street, we cannot clearly see its ground level because the ground surface falls abruptly into a little valley and woods: a stage 6 m below.

Programmatic Requirements
The program joins two different purposes: a house and an office, it is a place to both live and work. Although these two functions share the same space, it is as separate as possible.

Project Proposition
The different levels offered by the site were utilized to arrange the two main programs.

The street level was kept free of any enclosed space, it is a kind of "pilotis" with two different areas: the first one is on the ground, very close to the street, and the other one is aerial, as a roof terrace over the building. A bridge, made of steel, connects these two areas. The only entrance to the building is the bridge with its steel grid floor that leads over the open space: downstairs to the house or upstairs to the office.

The house is divided into two levels, both below the street level. Its spaces are integrated with the woods, valley, gardens, and pool located at the ground level. The house incorporates the outside nature indoors: a sliding glass door opens the living room into the terrace, creating one large space. The bedroom and the patios can also be integrated at the lower level.

From the street level, the office is located upstairs. Its dimensions, 3 m wide and 25 m long, making it look like a tube open at both extremities. Therefore, the windows offer new views: more landscape than patios, and more panoramic than an intimate space.

The "tube" only rests over two columns. Reinforced concrete supports the whole building. Besides its materials, concrete and glass, this house is essentially designed based on the site's geography and landscape. So few elements mean more concentration on the required work during its construction process. It makes it easier to control the budget and it help us focus on the necessary steps to build the house.

〈地理上の諸条件〉
この住宅がある敷地の最も顕著な特徴は，地形学的に下降していることである。道路からは，敷地の地盤面をはっきりと見ることはできない。地表が，6メートル下方にある小さな谷と森の中に，唐突に落ち込んでいるからである。

〈プログラム上の諸要件〉
プログラムは，住居とオフィスという二つの異なる目的をつなぎ合わせる。つまり，この住宅は住まう場であり，かつ仕事場にもなる。これら二つの機能は同じ空間を分かち合ってはいるが，可能な限り隔離されている。

〈計画案〉
異なるレベルによって，二つの主要プログラムを上手く配置できるよう，敷地が活用されることとなった。

道路レベルでは，閉じた空間がなく，二つの異なるエリアを備えた一種の「ピロティ」となっている。二つのエリアのうち，一つは地盤面にあり，道路に非常に近い。もう一つは空中にあり，建築を一面に覆うルーフテラスとなっている。スティール製のブリッジが，これら二つのエリアを繋いでいる。この建物の唯一の入口は，このスティール・グリッド・フロアのブリッジでオープンスペースを抜け，下階は住居へ，上階はオフィスへとつながっている。

住宅は二つのレベルに分割されており，どちらも道路レベルより下にある。その空間は，地上レベルにある森，谷，庭，プールと，一体化している。屋外の自然を屋内へと組み入れており，ガラスの引き戸を開けると，リビングルームがテラスへと開かれ，大きな一つの空間が生み出される。下階にある寝室とパティオもまた，一体化することが出来る。

オフィスは，道路レベルから見て上階に位置している。幅3メートル，長さ25メートルという大きさは，オフィスを，両端が開いている一本のチューブのように見せている。そのため，窓は，パティオよりも景観を，くつろいだ空間よりもパノラマを，と新たな眺望を見せている。

その「チューブ」は，わずか二本の柱の上に載っている。建物全体はRC造である。材料はコンクリートとガラスを用いる一方で，この住宅は，本質的に敷地の地形と景観に基づいてデザインされている。したがって少ないエレメントで済み，その分，工程上で求められる作業に重点をおける。これにより，予算コントロールがより簡便になり，必須となる各工程に対して集中して取り組めるのである。

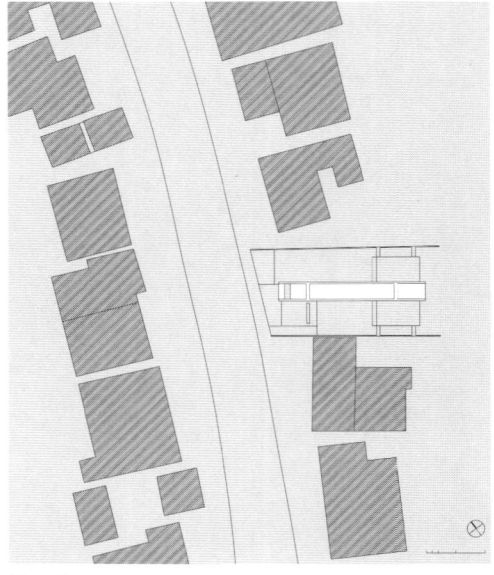

Site plan

Architects: spbr arquitetos—Angelo Bucci, Alvaro Puntoni, principals-in-charge;
Ciro Miguel, Fernando Bizarri, Juliana Braga, Maria Isabel Imbronito,
João Paulo Meirelles de Faria, project team
Client: Edward Magro
Consultants: Ibsen Pulleo Uvo, Ruy Bentes, structural; Klara Kaiser, landscape;
Alexsandro Bremenkamp, construction
Structural system: reinforced concrete
Major materials: concrete, glass and some pieces made of steel
Site area: 450 m²
Total floor area: 300 m²
Costs: US$ 300,000.00

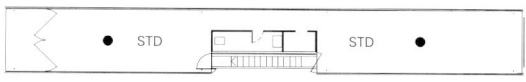

Level 102.95m (level 4)

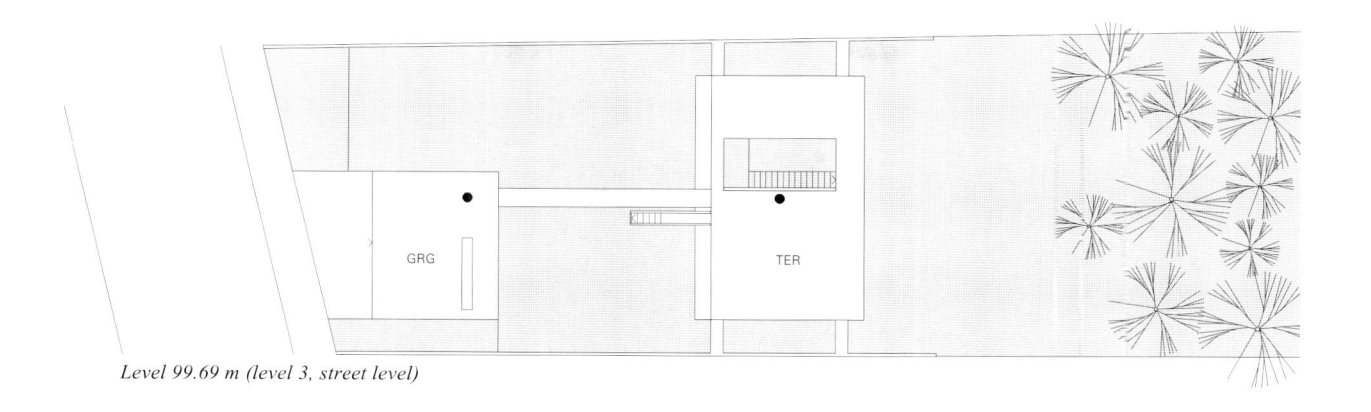

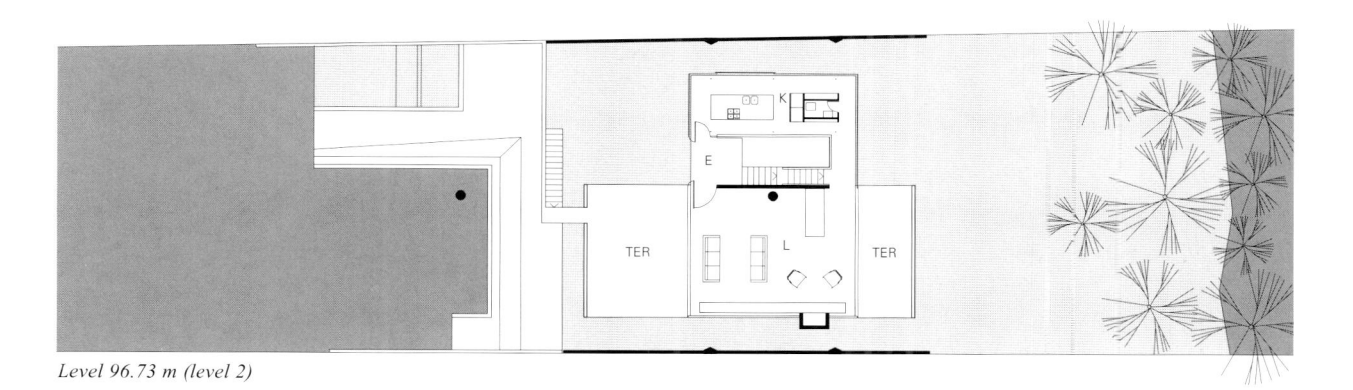

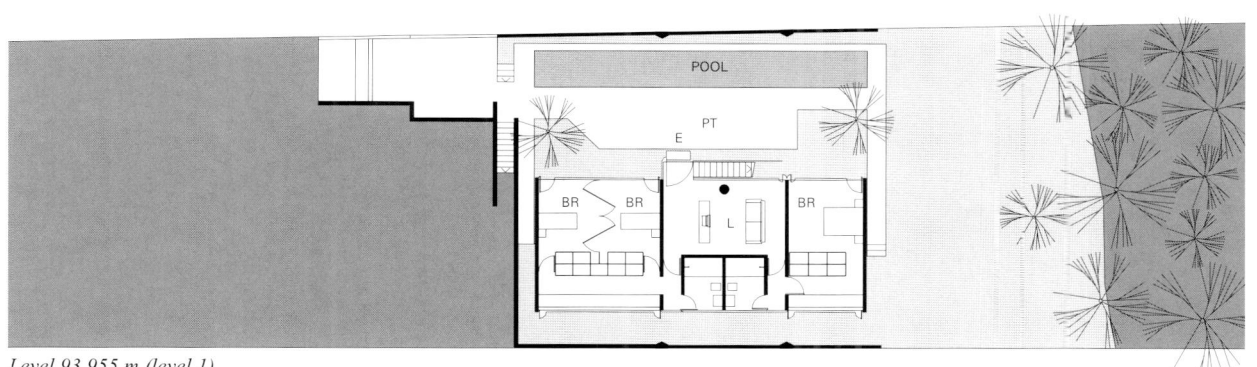

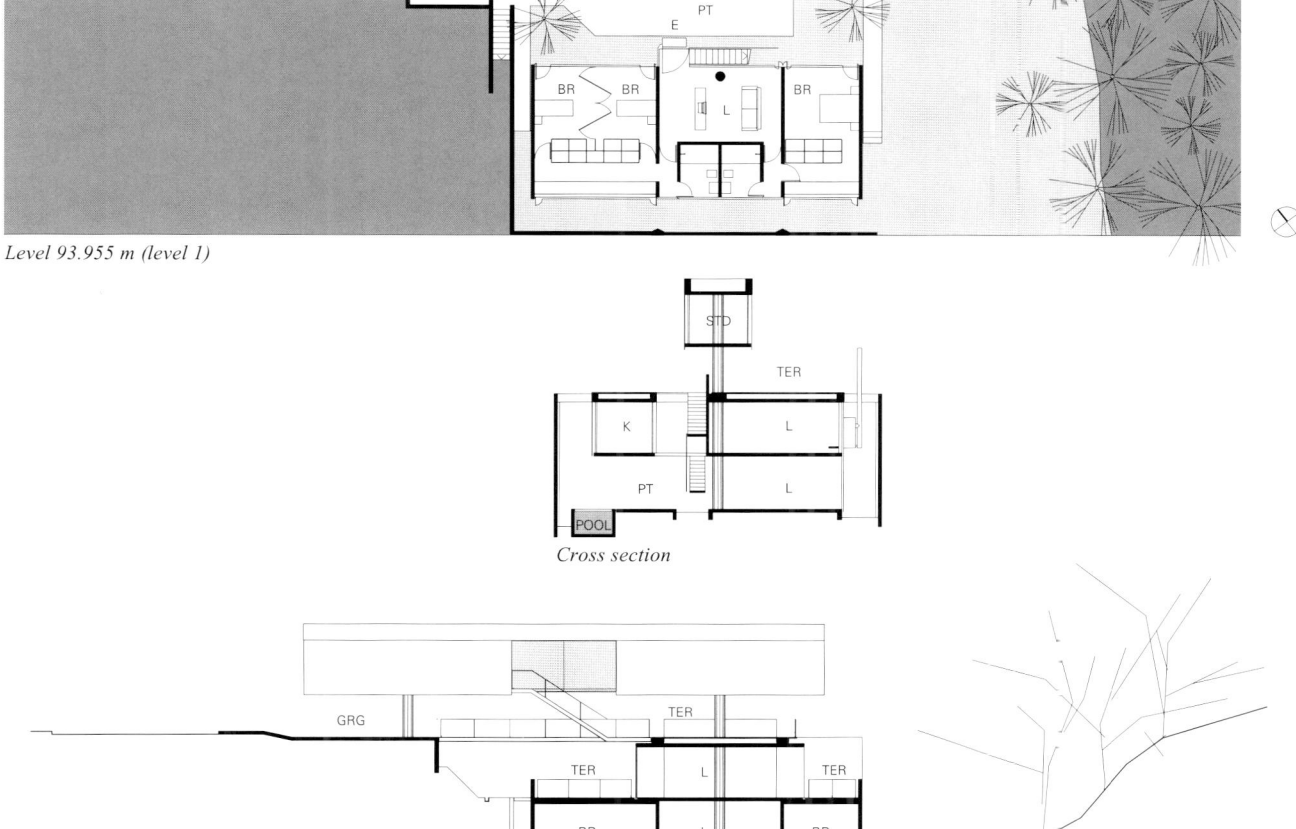

Level 99.69 m (level 3, street level)

Level 96.73 m (level 2)

Level 93.955 m (level 1)

Cross section

Longitudinal section

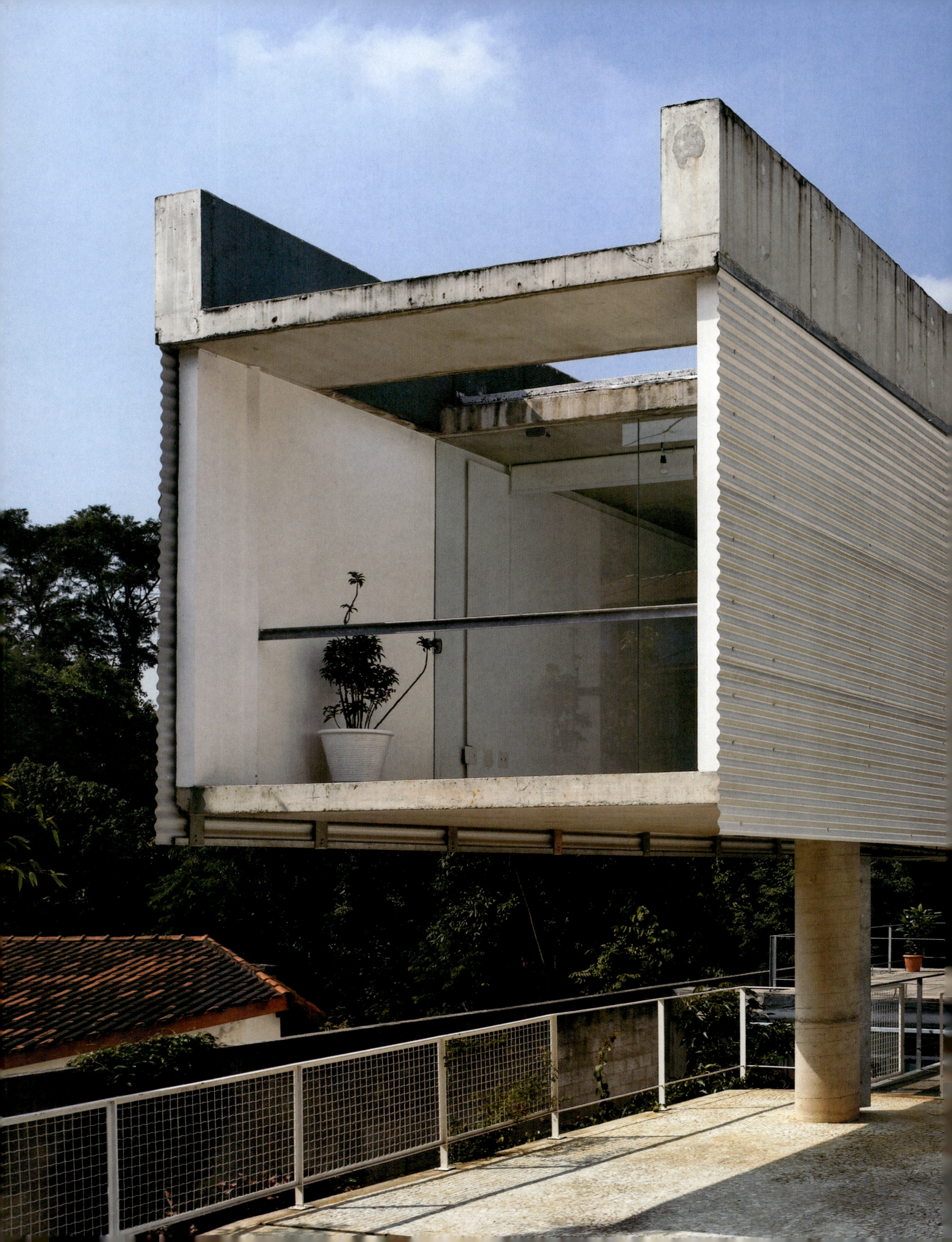

View of studio from garage on street level (level 3)　道路レベルのガレージよりスタジオを見る（レベル3）

View toward living room over terrace　テラス越しに居間方向を見る

Patio on level 1: each volume is piled rectangularly　　レベル1，パティオ：矩形のヴォリュームが交差しながら積み上がる

Bridge connecting house and garage: studio above ガレージと建物をつなぐブリッジ：上はスタジオ

View toward cantilevered kitchen on left: pool and bedrooms below　突き出した台所を左に見る：下はプールと寝室

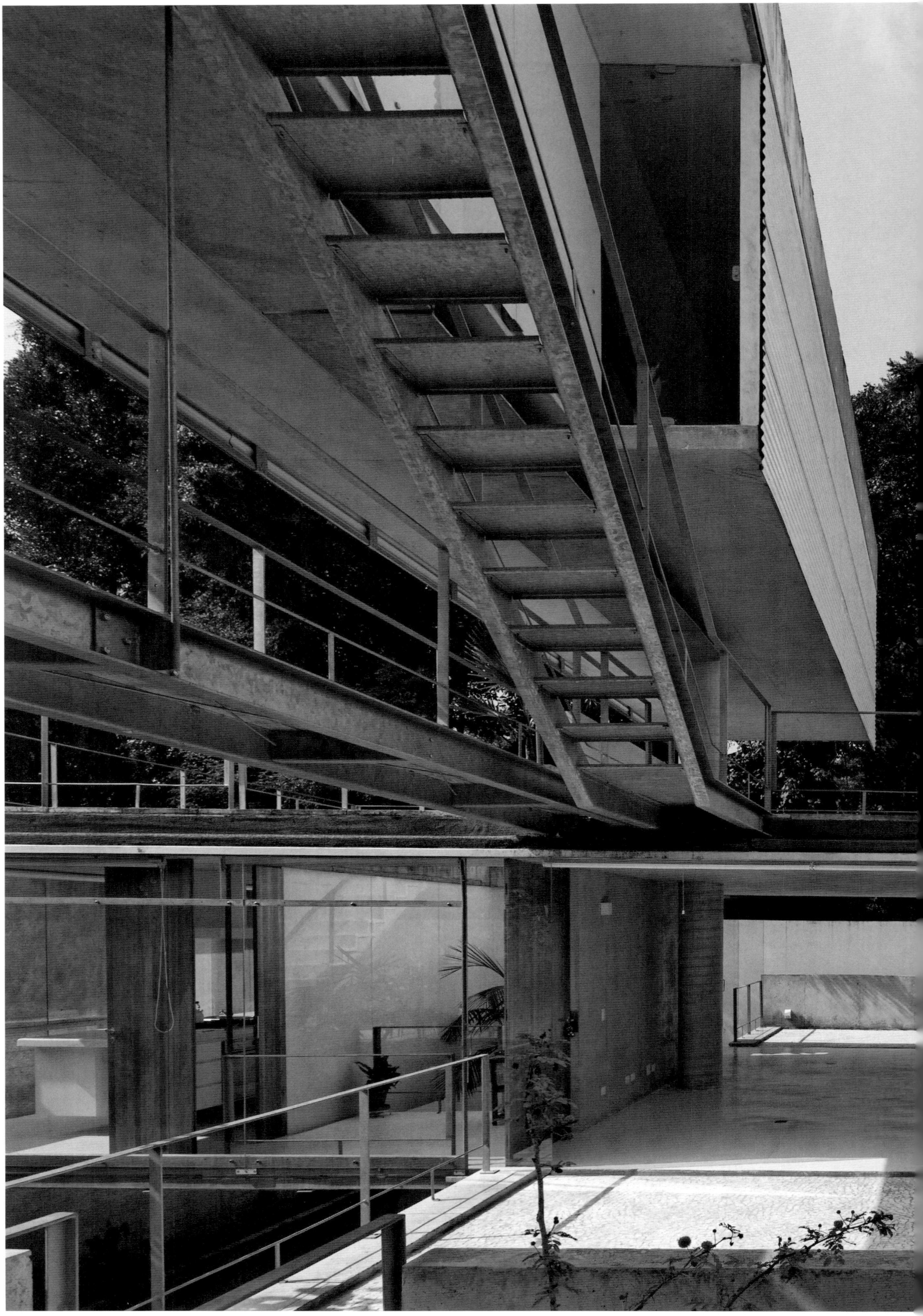

View toward living room on level 2　レベル2の居間を見る

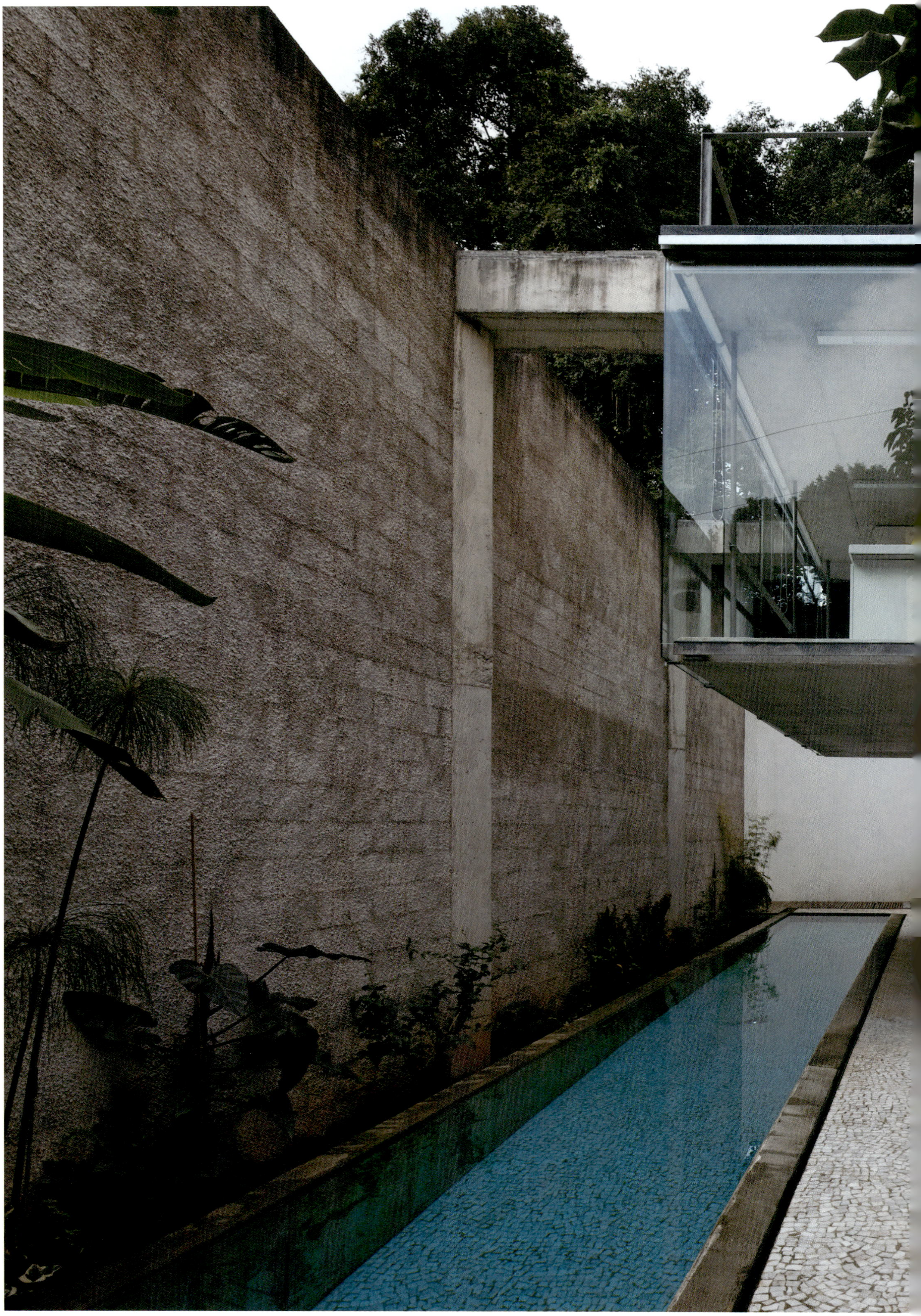

Patio on level 1: kitchen on center, bedrooms on right　レベル１，パティオ：正面は台所，右は寝室

Bridge to garage and staircase to studio　ガレージへつながるブリッジとスタジオへ上がる階段

Bridge: view toward terrace from garage　ブリッジ：ガレージよりテラスを見る

Living room on level 2　レベル 2，居間

73

△▽*Entrance on level 1*　レベル1，玄関

Bathroom 洗面所

Staircase to terrace on level 3
レベル3のテラスへ上がる階段

Kitchen 台所

ANDRADE MORETTIN

HOUSE RR

Itamambuca, Ubatuba, SP, Brazil
Design: 2006 Construction: 2007

Photos: Yoshio F.

View from southeast　南東より見る

East elevation: whole structure is raised 75 cm above the ground level　東面：全体が地面から75cm持ち上げられている

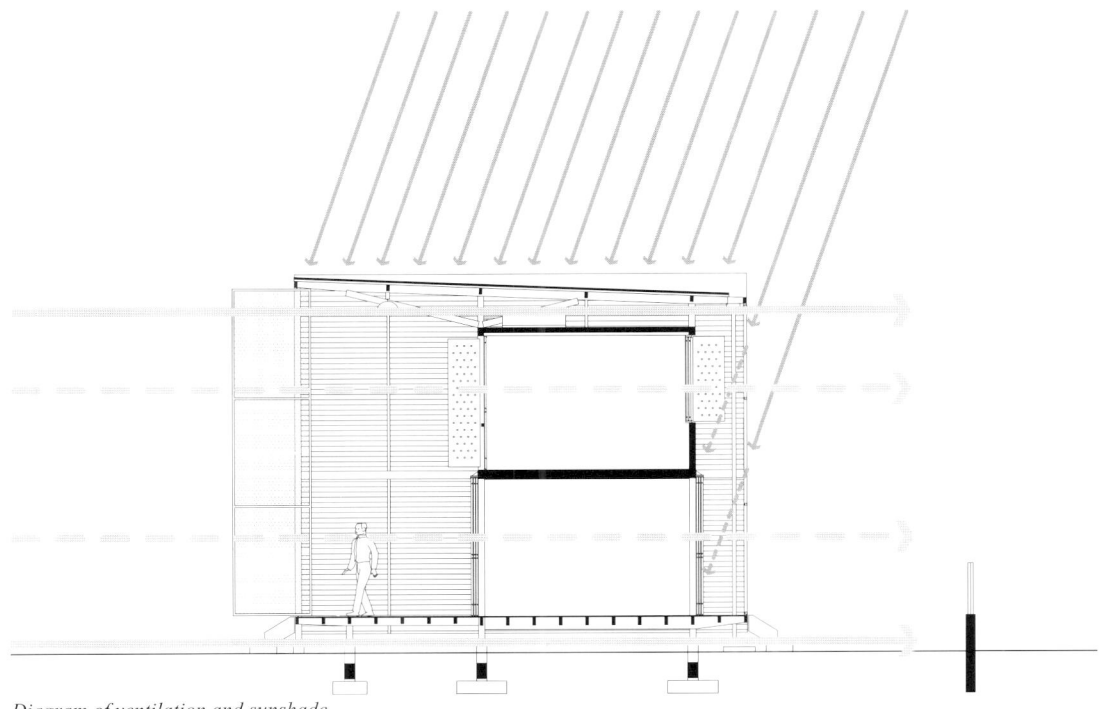

Diagram of ventilation and sunshade

Patio with glass fiber screen　ガラス繊維製の網戸が付いたパティオ

Patio: semi-outdoor area　半屋外のパティオ

View of patio over screen　スクリーン越しにパティオを見る

Site plan

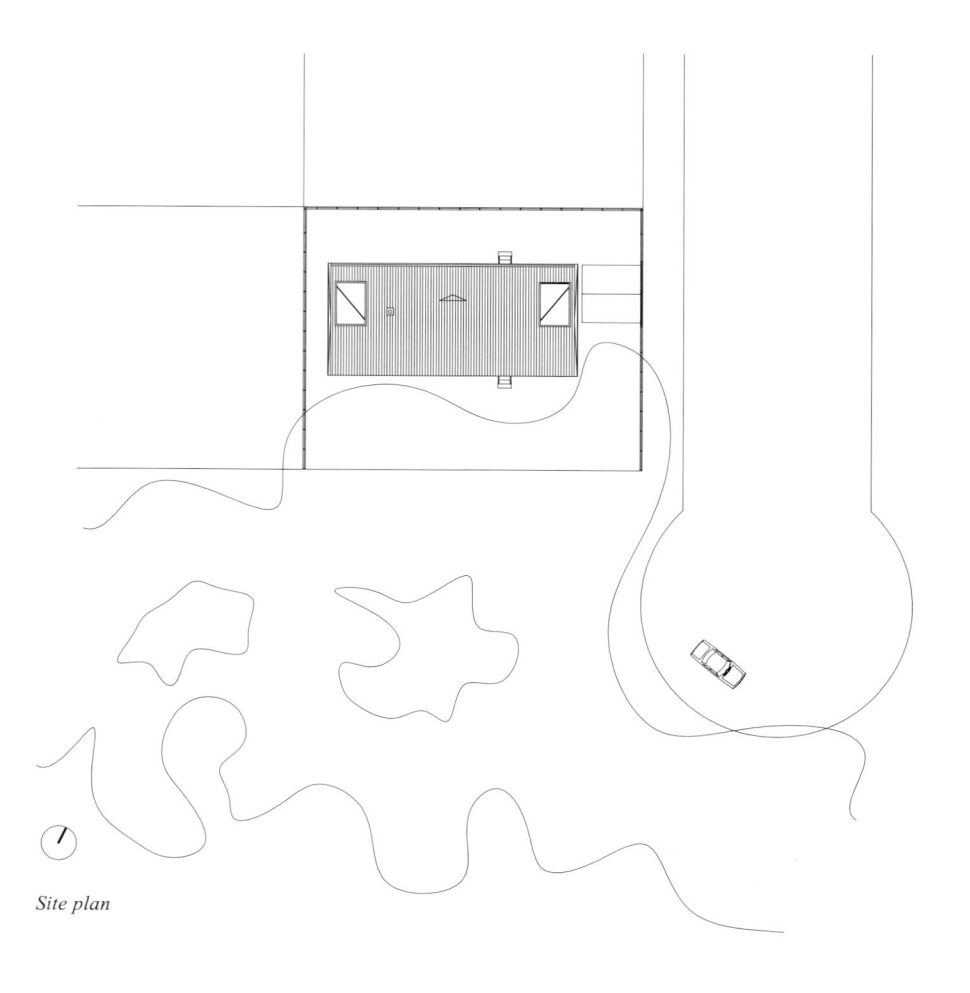

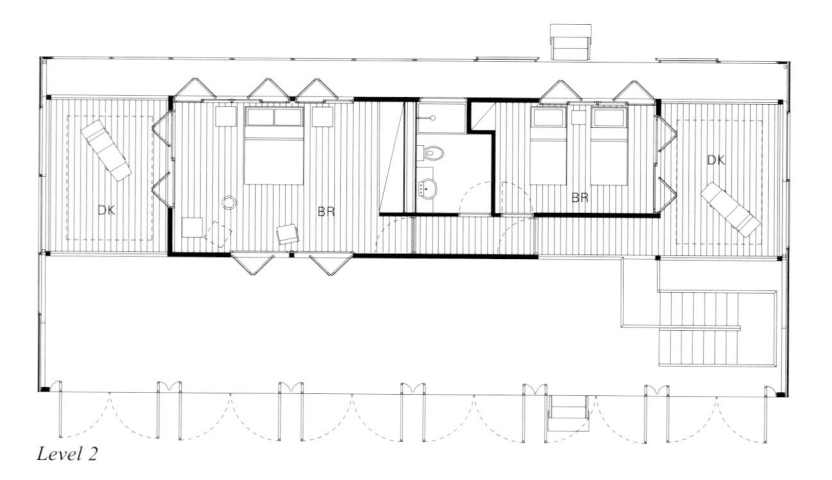

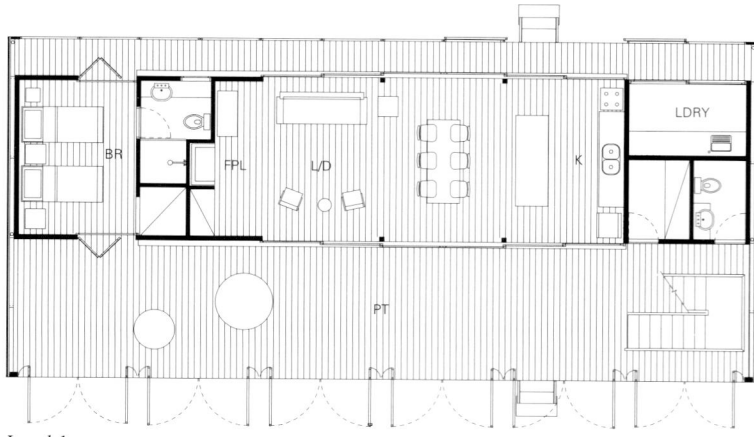

Level 2

Level 1

This summer house is situated only a few meters from the sea, on the north coast of the State of São Paulo, a place with exuberant vegetation and hot humid climate.

We began the project with the idea of a big shelter, a "shell", under which the actual living spaces would be located, protected from the intense sun and the frequent rains, however without blocking the permanent natural cross ventilation.

This roof at a height of six meters, with a surface of eighteen by eight meters, was built using a pre-fabricated timber structure with galvanized steel joints. The lateral and top faces are made of steel cladding with EPS filling.

On the two large facades of the house, opening generously to the scenery, panels of glass fiber mosquito screens with PVC coating were installed, pivoting or sliding, with the intention of creating an external membrane, capable of keeping the insects out, without creating an obstacle for the ocean view and wind.

The whole structure is elevated 75 cm above ground level, supported by concrete pillars cast on site. All other components used in the construction are pre-fabricated and were simply mounted in place on the construction site.

The adopted constructive system, besides reducing assembly time and errors, assured a dry construction site, with little generation of waste and low environmental impact.

Bioclimatic Performance/Environmental Performance

Based on the belief that good design can reduce the carbon footprint more than technological supplements and considering the quality of the environment (humid tropical region), shade and ventilation are understood as essential strategic resources to achieve good bioclimatic performance.

Instead of using expensive green technologies, this house seeks to respond to the ecological issues basically by means of reduction, with economical use of materials: "Lightness".

Based on passive principles, the building demands a minimal consumption of energy for operation and maintenance.

Materials with a small mass or thermal inertia were employed, avoiding the accumulation of heat during the day, since the nights are equally hot. The use of bright surfaces also minimizes the absorption of solar radiation.

The possibility of producing clean energy on the site, however, is not abandoned. Depending on the financial situation of the owners, photovoltaic panels can be installed on the roof.

この夏の家は，サンパウロ州の北部海岸に面し，浜辺からほんの数メートル離れた，植物が繁茂する高温多湿な場所にある。

私たちはこのプロジェクトを一つの大きなシェルター，その下には，強い陽射しと頻繁に降る雨から守られるが，常に自然通気を妨げられることのない生活空間を収めた"シェル"という考えからスタートさせた。

6メートルの高さにあり，18メートル×8メートルの面を持つ屋根は，プレファブの木構造に亜鉛メッキ鋼のジョイントを用いて建ち上げ，側面と上面はEPS断熱材を充填した鋼板で被覆。

景色に向けて広く開放された建物の二側面には，PVCコーティングしたガラス繊維製の回転あるいはスライドする蚊除けスクリーン・パネルが，海の眺めや通風を妨げずに虫を除けることのできる，外側の被膜として装填されている。

建物全体は，敷地に打ち込まれたコンクリート柱に支持されて，地上から75センチ持ち上げられている。使用されているその他の部材のすべては，プレファブで，現場で簡単に据え付けられた。

採用された建築システムは，組み立てに要する時間とミスを減らすことの他に，乾燥した建設現場，廃棄物の産出の少なさ，環境への影響の低さを保証するものであった。

〈生物気候学的性能／環境性能〉
優れたデザインは，技術的装置を補足するよりも二酸化炭素を減らすことができるという信念に基づき，敷地環境の特徴（多湿な熱帯地方）も考えながら，日影と通気が，高い生物気候学的性能を達成するために必須条件であると判断した。

高価なグリーン・テクノロジーを使う代わりに，基本的に材料の経済的使用つまり"軽くすること"と共に縮小することによってエコロジカルな問題に応えようとつとめている。

パッシブな原則に基づいて，設備の稼働とメンテナンスのためのエネルギー消費を最小限にすることが必要である。

夜間も同じように暑いので，日中の蓄熱を避けて建物のかさを小さくし，熱不活性な材料を採用した。キラキラ光る面材の使用もまた太陽の放射熱の吸収を最小限に抑えてくれる。

しかし，敷地でクリーン・エネルギーをつくりだす可能性を放棄するものではない。オーナーの経済状況に応じて，光起電パネルを屋根に設置することもできる。

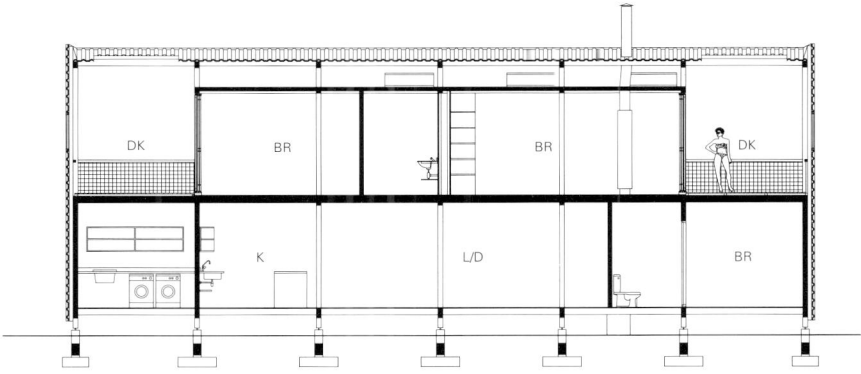

Longitudinal section

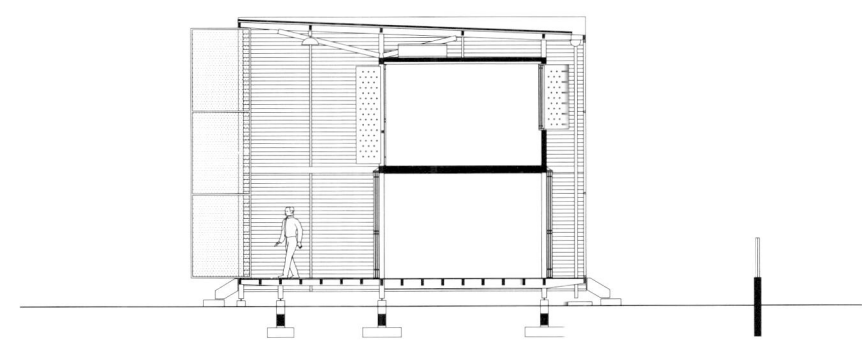

Cross section

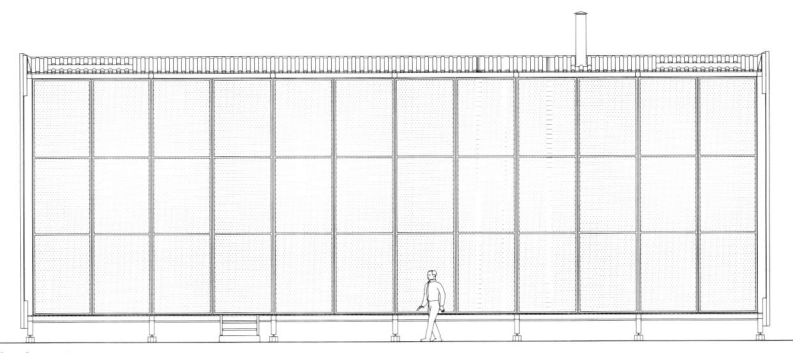

North elevation

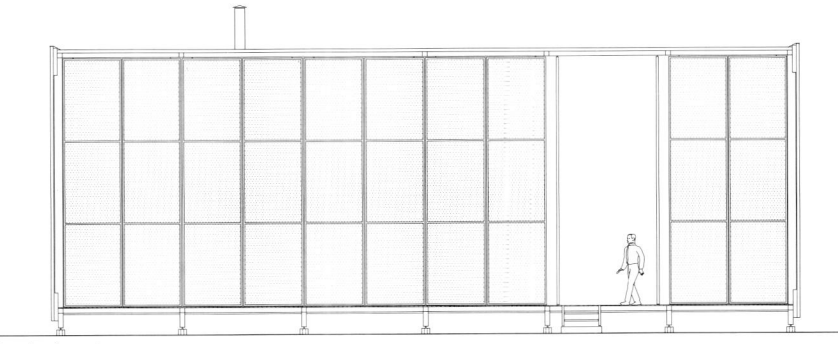

South elevation

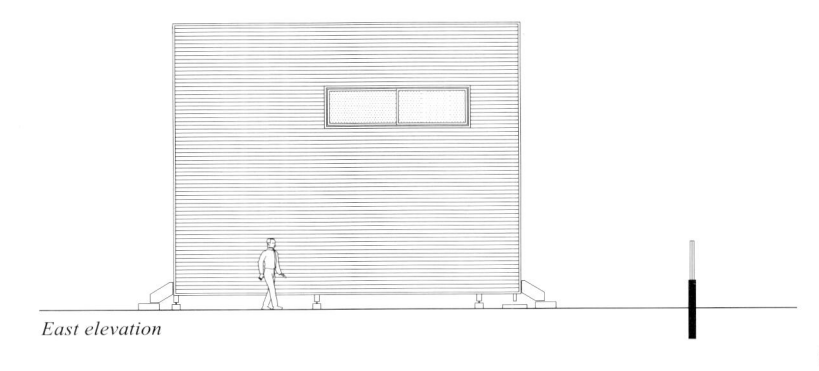

East elevation

View from living room toward patio　居間よりパティオを見る

Dining room open to patio　パティオとひとつながりの食堂

Deck on level 2　2階デッキ

Chimeny and wooden fixture　スティール・シートが巻かれた煙突と木の建具

View toward bedroom from deck　デッキより寝室を見る

83

△▽Patio パティオ

Architects: Andrade Morettin Arquitetos Associados—Vinícius Andrade, Marcelo Morettin, principals-in-charge; Merten Nefs, project cordinator; Marcelo Maia Rosa, Marcio Tanaka, Marina Mermelstein, Renata Andrulis, project team
Consultants: Helio Olga—Ita Construtora, structural; Pedro Negri, foundation; Nilton José Maziero, electrical
General contractor: Vicente Ganzelevitch
Structural system: timber with galvanized steel joints
Major materials: OSB Panels, dry-wall plaster boards, mosquito screen facades/glass fiber screen with PVC coating in steel frames, thermo-acoustic steel cladding with EPS filling (roof and side facades)
Site area: 500 m²
Built area: 160 m²
Total floor area: 220 m²

Patio　パティオ

Upward view of patio　パティオ見上げ

85

MMBB ARQUITETOS

VILA ROMANA RESIDENCE AND STUDIO

São Paulo, SP, Brazil
Design: 2004–05 Construction: 2005–06

Photos: Yoshio F.

Upward view from street on south 南側道路より見る

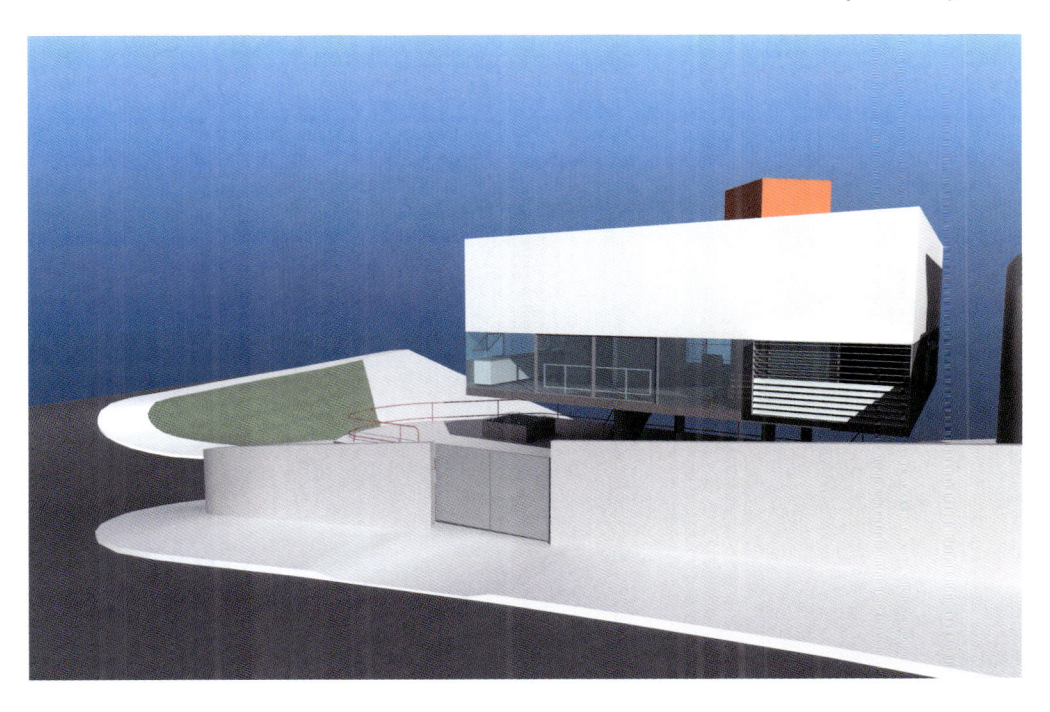

The design of the Vila Romana Residence is derived from the twin imperatives of topography and usage.

It is situated on a corner plot with views of the town's principal valley, with a drop of 10 meters from one side of the plot to the other.

The first question to be tackled was that of creating an artificial terrain that would allow for easy transit around the external areas and their use for day-to-day activities. The landscaping was determined by the creation of these areas.

The second question was that of the residence's dual usage. The building houses not only the residence but also the working studio of the artist owner.

The strategy adopted was to divide the building into two autonomous blocks. In contact with the terrain is the studio block, partly embedded in the hill and illuminated only by an overhead opening. Its interior is divided by a series of walls which serve as supports for the works to be created there.

Suspended above the terrain is the block containing the residency itself, open to the views that surround it. Its internal layout is designed to facilitate integration and fluidity between separate sectors for living, sleeping, cooking and the service area.

Between the two blocks, on the slab that forms the roof of the studio, a large veranda has been created, partly in shadow. Another space, uncovered, occupies the slab over the residential block as a sky deck, increasing the total external ground area.

The suspended block is supported on only four points, with prominent overhangs. The two solid slabs that support it are constructed from apparent prestressed concrete. A further layer of concrete conceals the steel reinforcing elements. This concrete and the window system form the facade of the building.

The concrete slabs, once polished, form the floor of the interior environment, with no need for additional surfacing.

Conical niches in the concrete allow for the direct installation of lighting, with no need for additional fixtures.

It is this succession of constructional features that defines the project as a whole.

この住宅のデザインは，地形と用途という2つの回避不可能な要素から生まれている。

角地にあり，町の主要な谷を見晴らし，敷地の片側はその反対側から10メートル落ちている。

取り組まねばならない最初の課題は，屋外エリア全体を簡単に行き来でき，日常の活動に支障なく使える人工地盤をつくることである。景観構成はこれらのエリアをつくりだすことによって決定される。

第2の課題は，この家の二重の使い方にある。住居スペースばかりでなく，アーティストであるオーナーが仕事をするスタジオも必要としている。

自立する2つの棟へ建物を分割する戦略をとった。土地と接してスタジオ棟を配置し，その一部を丘のなかに埋め込み，頭上の開口部からのみ採光する。内部空間はそこでの創作活動を助ける一連の壁で分割される。

地上高く持ち上げた棟は居住空間で，周囲の風景に向けて開かれる。内部空間は，リビング，寝室，調理，及びサービスエリアで分けられた各領域間のまとまりや流れをシンプルなものにするように構成されている。

2つの棟の間，スタジオの屋根を構成するスラブ上には，一部に日除けを付けた広いベランダがつくられる。もう一つ別の覆いが無い屋外スペースは，住居棟を覆うスラブをスカイ・デッキとすることで，屋外の地盤面の総面積を増加させる。

4点のみで支えられた住居棟は，吊られたように印象的に張り出している。棟を支持する2つのソリッドなスラブは，打ち放しのプレストレス・コンクリートである。その上に重ねられたコンクリートがスティールの補強要素を隠す。このコンクリートと窓のシステムが建物のファサードを形成する。

一度磨かれたコンクリート・スラブが内部空間の床に使用され，追加の磨き仕上げは必要ない。コンクリートにとられた円錐形のニッチに照明を直接設置できるので，取り付け装置の追加は不要である。

こうした一連の建設面での特徴がプロジェクト全体を規定する。

View from street on southeast　南東側道路より見る

Architects: MMBB Arquitetos—
Fernando de Mello Franco, Marta Moreira, Milton Braga, principals-in-charge;
Ana Carina Costa, Márcia Terazaki, Marina Sabino, Marina Acayaba, Thiago Rolemberg, Rodrigo Brancher, project team
Client: Iran do Espírito Santo
Consultants: Kurkdjian & Fruchtengarten Engenheiros Associados, structural;
Procion Engenharia, mechanical; MMBB Arquitetos, Iran do Espírito Santo, interior;
Iran do Espírito Santo, Ana Cintra, landscape;
Ceppolina Engenheiros Consultores, foundations
Program: single family residence and artist's studio
Structural system: reinforced and prestressed concrete
Major materials: concrete
Site area: 500 m²
Built area: 290 m²
Total floor area: 435 m²
Costs: US$ 425,000.00

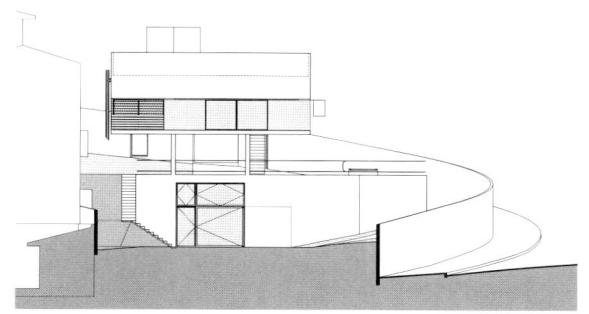

Northwest elevation

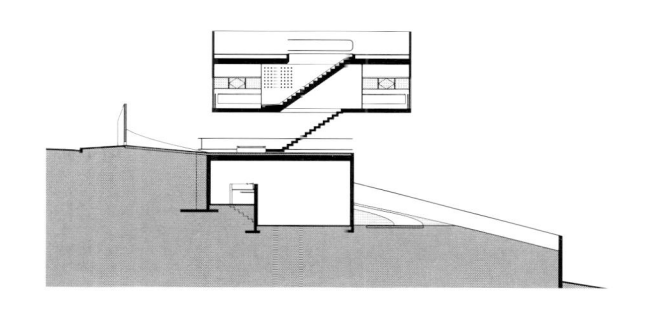

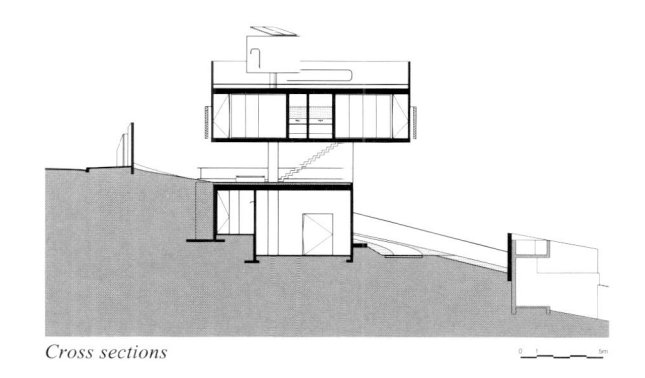

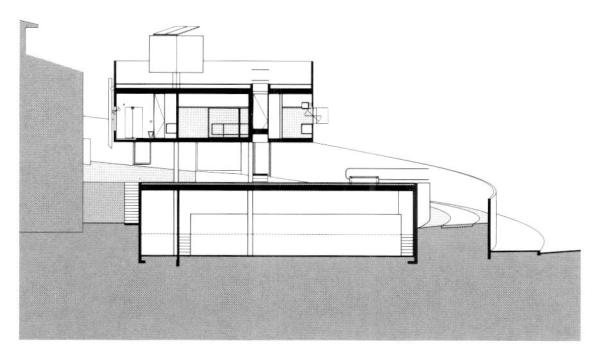

Section

Cross sections

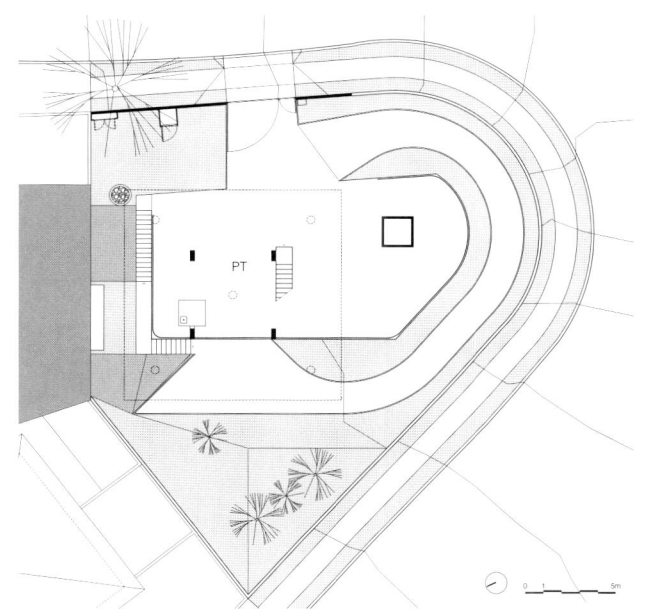

Ground level

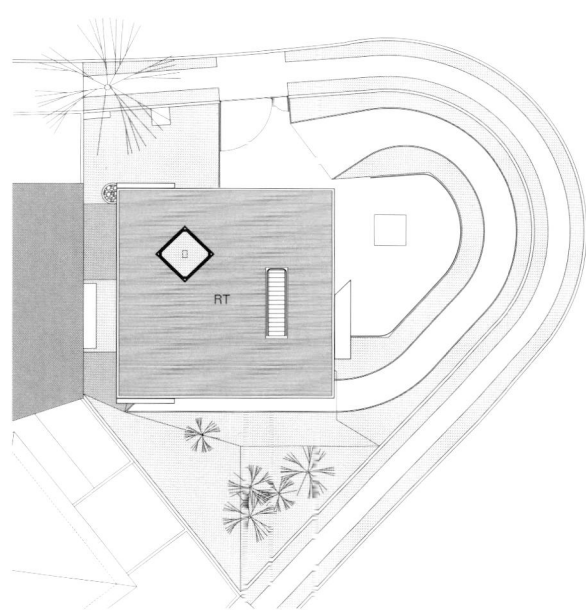

Roof

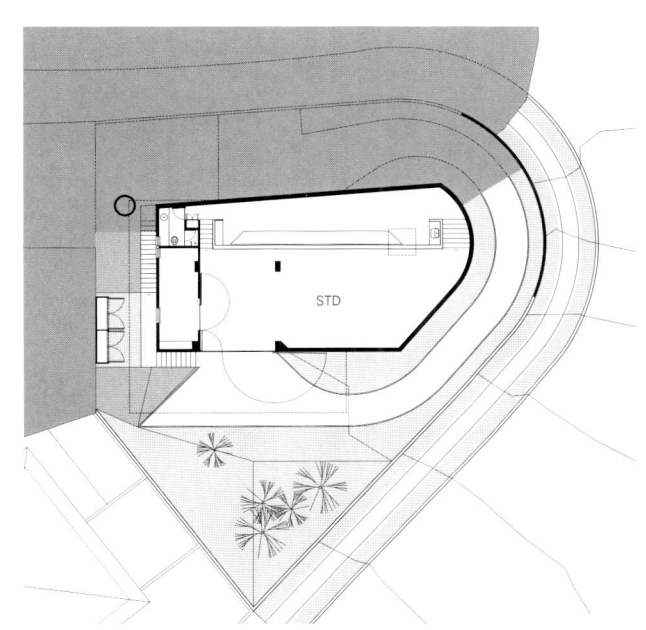

Lower level

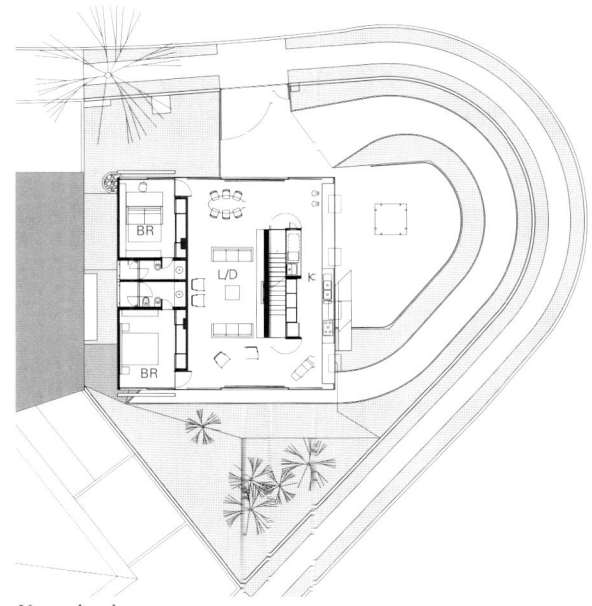

Upper level

89

Patio　パティオ

Patio: aperture leads natural light toward studio below　パティオ：開口部を通して下階のスタジオに自然光が射し込む

Staircase to house entrance 住宅玄関へ上がる階段△▽

Living room: view toward bedroom　居間：寝室方向を見る

Staircase to roof: kitchen on left, living room on right　屋上へ上がる階段室：左は台所，右は居間

West end of kitchen: corner without supporting column　台所西端：支持柱の無い角部

Panorama from kitchen　台所からの眺め

Staircase to roof　屋上へ上がる階段

Bedroom　寝室

Dining room 　食堂

Living room 　居間

Roof terrace with water tank
ウォーター・タンクのあるルーフ・テラス

95

△▽ *Studio on lower level*　下階にあるスタジオ

Studio on lower level　下階にあるスタジオ△▽

NITSCHE ARQUITETOS

HOUSE IN IPORANGA

Iporanga, Guarujá, SP, Brazil
Design: 2004–05 Construction: 2005–06

Photos: Yoshio F.

Approach アプローチ

View from terrace: living/dining room on lower level. Bedrooms on upper level　テラスより見る：下階は居間／食堂。上階は寝室

Iporanga House, is located in Iporanga a condominium for summer houses on São Paulo's coast, approximately 120 km east from the capital. This condo is inside a very well preserved and protected area of the original Atlantic Rainforest. The exuberance of this native forest has taken the client to demand a house that occupied the minimum as possible of the ground (lot) surface. But at the same time he wanted it to be large and comfortable, and asked for 5 suites, one for the couple, one for each of his 3 sons and one for guests, which demanded not less the 400 m² to be built.

So we decided to split the program in 3 levels: a suspended volume, wood structured for the 5 suites, so they would be on the trees' crown/top; a plan, the concrete slab elevated from the ground to support all of the program social activities, living, dinning room the kitchen and the swimming pool; and underneath it, on ground level there is a small enclosed area for services. A small accommodation for a house keeper couple, a laundry and a depository.

The wood frame volume is the "private" part of the house, therefore on the street side it is enclosed by opaque boards (made of wood and covered on both faces with a cement slab), glass panels along with a nylon curtain, and on the forest side, aluminum sliding doors opening the rooms to a common veranda. This volume creates a shadow on the slab, and we used that shadow for the social area. This "middle" floor is almost an open space, protected on all sides by transparent tempered glass sliding panels, so the forest can be seen at all times. The intention was to minimize the difference between inner and outside space, making it work all as one integrated area.

The structural concept of the house was inspired by small brook bridges typical from this littoral area. Rising from the foundation in humid soil, concrete columns support the steel beams which support the wood frame.

We tried to make the construction an assembling of parts more than an in loco process, concerning less waste at the building site, more agility and proper use of industrialized materials.

州都から東に約120キロ，サンパウロ州の海岸沿いの町イポランガにある，夏の家で構成されたコンドミニアム内に建てられた住宅。コンドミニアムは，原始の大西洋岸熱帯雨林内の非常によく保存され，保護されているエリアに位置し，その自然のままの森の豊かさは，クライアントに接地面積を最小限に抑えた家にしたいと思わせた。しかし同時に彼は，この家が，広く，快適なものにしたいと望み，クライアント夫妻，3人の息子たち，そしてゲストのために計5室の寝室を含めた，全体で400平米を下らない建築面積を求めたのである。

このため，プログラムを3つのレベルに分割して配置することに決めた。5つの寝室が並ぶ木造のヴォリュームは，高く支持され，梢に面することになる。次は居間，食堂，台所，水泳プールなど，共有の活動領域をすべて配した，地上から持ち上げられたコンクリート・スラブの階。そしてその下の地上階には，サービス諸室を収めた小さな囲まれたエリアがくる。ここには管理人夫妻の小さな居室，ランドリー，倉庫がある。

木造軸組構法のヴォリュームは，家の"私的領域"であるため，道路側は不透明なボード（木製で，両面をセメント板で被覆）とナイロン・カーテンの付いたガラス・パネル，森に面しては共有ベランダに向かって部屋を開放できるアルミ製の引き戸で構成されている。この木造ヴォリュームは，下のコンクリート・スラブ上に日影をつくりだし，この日影が共有エリアのために活用される。この"中間の"階はほとんどがオープンスペースで，側面すべてが透明な強化ガラスのスライディング・パネルで囲まれ，常時，森を見ることができる。これは屋内と屋外の差異を最小限にして，全体を一体感のあるエリアにつくりあげようと意図したものである。

建物の構造を考える上で，この沿岸地帯に典型的な，小さな流れを架け渡す橋からヒントを得た。湿地の土壌に打ち込まれた基礎から立ち上がるコンクリート柱が，木造フレームを支持する鉄骨梁を支える。

現場での無駄を省き，工業化された材料をより敏速に適切に使うように考えながら，現場で作業をするというよりは，パーツの組み立てとして工事が行えるように試みた。

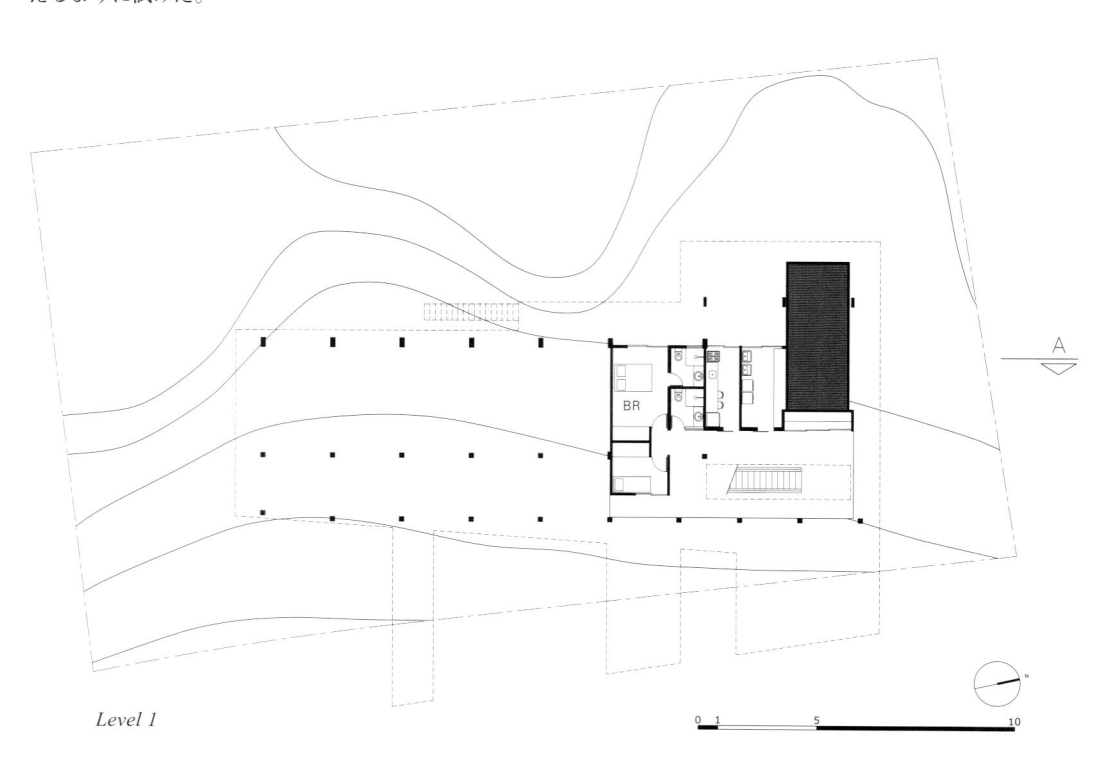

Architects: Nitsche Arquitetos Associados—
Lua Nitsche, principal-in-charge;
Lua and Pedro Nitsche, design architects;
Renata Cupini, Suzana Barboza,
Mariana Simas, project team
Consultants: Ita construtura, structural (wood);
L Camargo engenharia de projetos, foundation and structural (concrete); Grau Engenharia, electrical, plumbing and air condition; Cia de iluminação, lighting; Janos Biezók, stairs and kitchen tables; Paysage jardins internos e externos, landscape
General contractor: Tecsa Engenharia
Program: summer house
Structural system: rising from foundation in humid soil, concrete columns support steel beams which support wood frame
Major materials: wood, concrete and steel
Site area: 1,220 m²
Built area: 554 m², total area including terraces; 252 m², inside area
Total floor area: 801 m²

Level 1

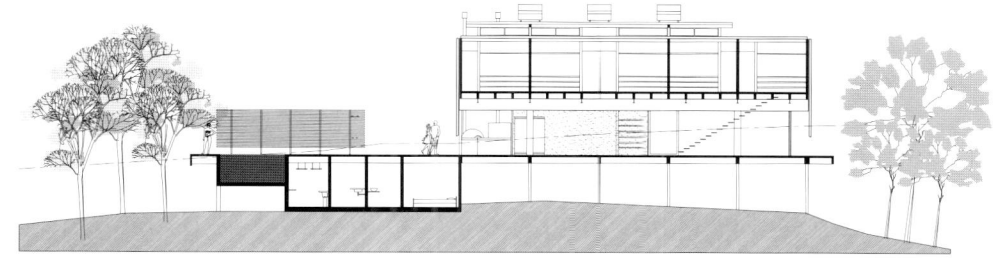

Section

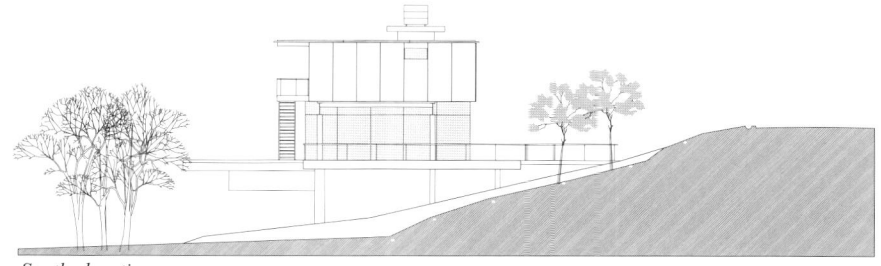

South elevation

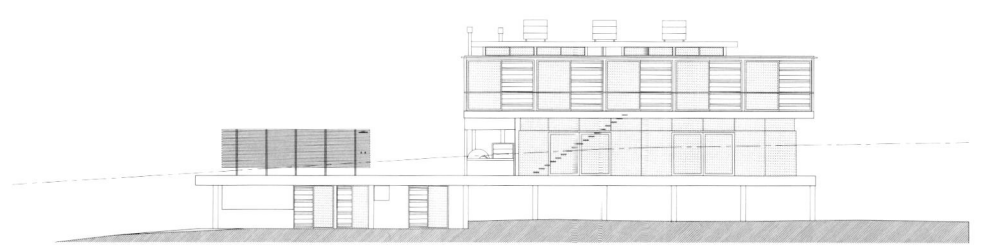

West elevation

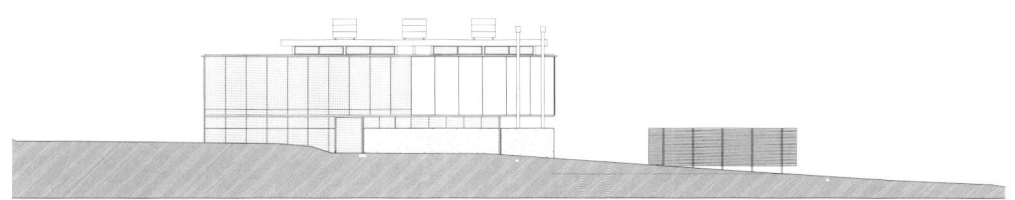

East elevation

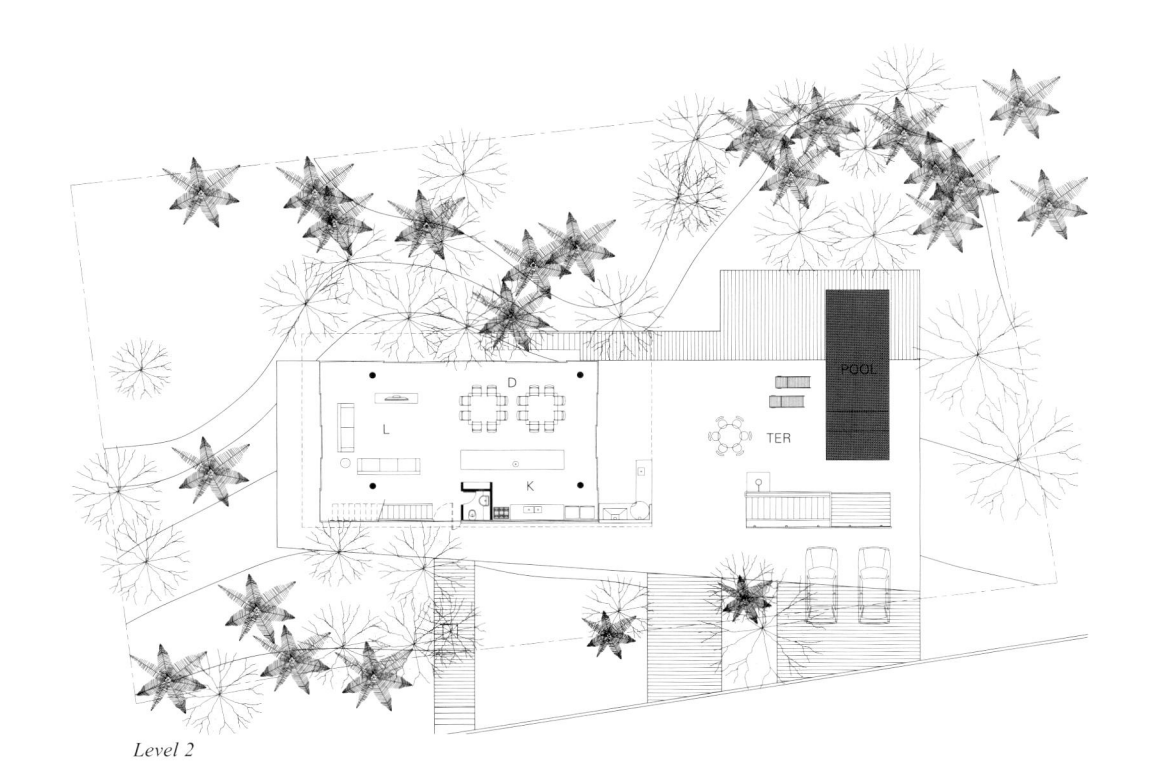

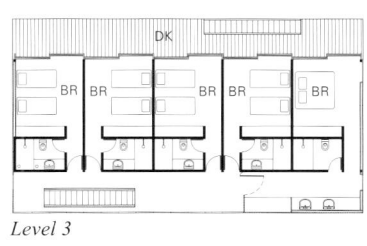

Level 2

Level 3

101

View toward corner from terrace. Kitchen and dining room is open to terrace　テラスより角部を見る。テラスに開かれた台所／食堂

East side: view toward staircase over glazed wall 東面：窓越しに階段を見る

Deck along bedrooms on level 3 3階寝室脇のデッキ

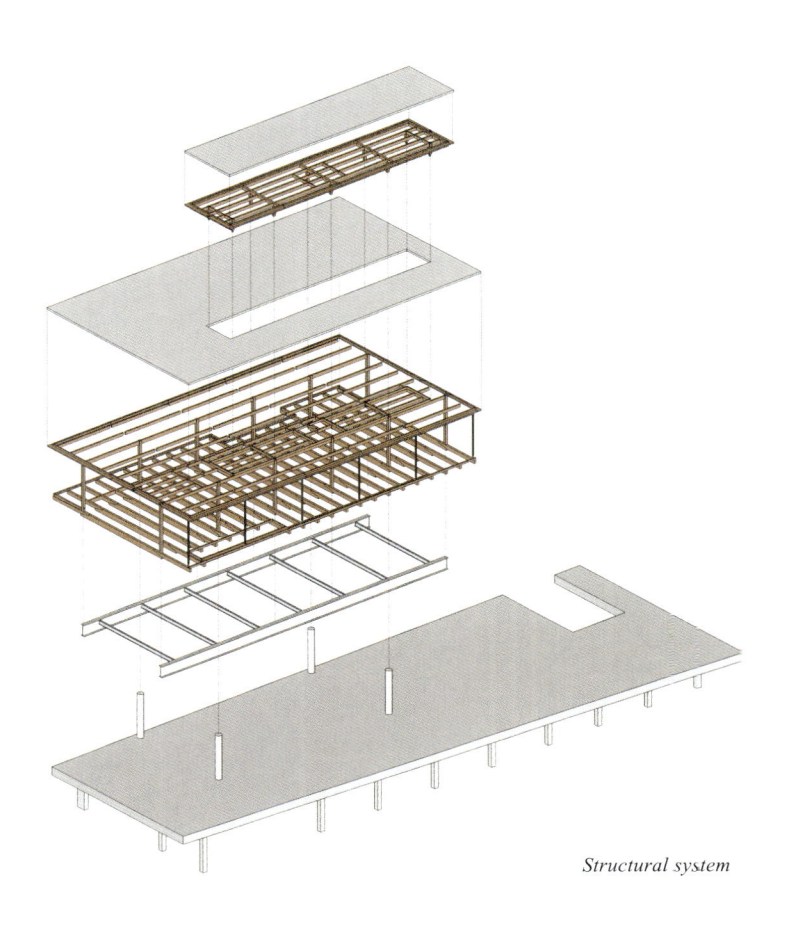

Structural system

103

East elevation 東面

Outside staircase along dining room　食堂脇の外階段

View from terrace toward kitchen and dining room　テラスより台所／食堂を見る

Kitchen and dining room　台所／食堂

Staircase to level 3　3階へつづく階段

Kitchen and dining room: view toward terrace　台所／食堂：テラスを見る

Corridor on level 3　3階廊下

Corridor on level 3　3階廊下

Deck on level 3　3階デッキ

Kitchen and dining room, living room behind　台所／食堂，奥に居間

//
GESTO AMBIENTAL

"POUSO ALTO" HOUSE

São Sebastião, SP, Brazil
Design: 2002–03 Construction: 2003–04

◁△*Corner: curved steels as roof support slabs*　角部：湾曲したスティール材が屋根となり，スラブを支える

Bridge connecting terrace and living room　テラスと居間をつなぐブリッジ

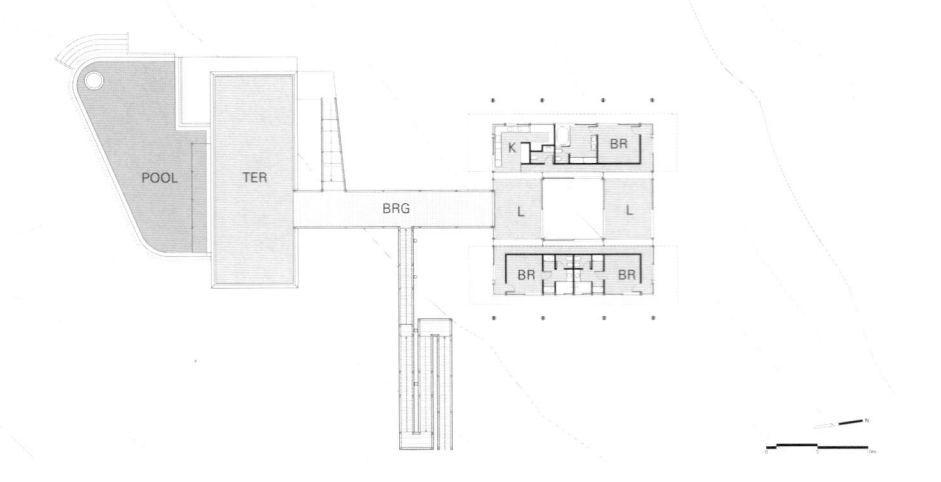

Plan

This residence is the result of an eco-lodge project that has been planed in the northern coast of the state of São Paulo, Brazil.

The site is a strategic position, geographically and environmentally, because it's the intersection between the dense urbanized areas among the coast and the pressured Atlantic forest, the "Serra do Mar" State Park. It represents a buffer zone and it's extremely important for the maintenance of the biodiversity in the preserved areas. A strategic planning among those areas is crucial for the success of Parks and Reserves in Brazil. The residence is located on a land contiguous to an ecological lodge site and it's the first experiment of the whole enterprise.

This project is a result of a multidisciplinary study. It is made by a diversity of professionals to diagnostic the complexity of the site and brings a proposition that would answer the habit necessity, the understanding of the natural systems in the area and to cooperate with conservation of forest.

Looking for the references of civilizations that have the knowledge of living in the nature a vast study is made of the constructions of the Brazilian indigenous tribes. This investigation brought the designing elements of sustainable relations for this contemporary and comfortable house. Seeking less impact on the natural environment the building "fly" above the ground. It interferes gently on the landscape and allows the connectivity of the vegetation and the fauna from bellow.

Been elevated above the ground permit the observer to interact with the different levels of the forest and to be closer to the canopy where most of the biodiversity is.

This project try to discuss the structures of our forests and desire to bring reflections of sustainability for our cities. The living place, as a unit of the urban system, needs to be reconsidered and reviewed. It represents a challenge for its significance as urban and human perspective.

この住宅はブラジル，サン・パウロ州の北部海岸に進められてきたエコ・ロッジ計画の成果である。

敷地は海岸線のなかでも高密度に都市化された地域と"セーラ ド・マール（海岸山脈）"州立公園の大西洋岸森林帯がせめぎあう交差部にあるため，地形の点でも環境の点でも重要な位置を占めている。そこは緩衝地域を代表し，その保護地区内の生物多様性を維持することが不可欠であり，これらの地域内での戦略的計画立案はブラジルに於ける公園と保存の成功にとって極めて重要である。この住宅は，エコロジカルなロッジ・サイトに続く土地に位置を占め，サイト全体で最初の試みとなる。

プロジェクトはいくつかの専門分野を結集したスタディから生まれた。それは敷地の複雑さを診断分析するための多彩な専門家によって組み立てられ，この地域の自然システムの理解，森の保全と協力するために必要な動植物の習性に答えるだろう提案が投入されている。

自然のなかでの生活の知恵を備えた文明に参考例を探して，ブラジルの先住民族の建物についての広範なスタディが行われた。この調査は，この現代的で快適な住宅に，持続可能性（サステイナビリティ）に関わるデザイン要素をもたらした。自然環境への影響を少なくするために，建物は地表を"舞うように"立ち上がっている。それは穏やかに風景に干渉し，下に広がる植生や動物相とのつながりを容認する。

地上から持ち上げられているので，この家のなかで観察者は，森とさまざまな高さで交流し，生物多様性の大部分が存在する樹葉の天蓋へ近づくことができる。

このプロジェクトは，私たちの森の構造を論じる試みであり，私たちの都市に持続可能性を反映させたいという願望である。都市システムの一単位としての生活の場は，再考され，見直される必要がある。それは，都市と人間の全体像としてのその重要性に対する一つのチャレンジを提示する。

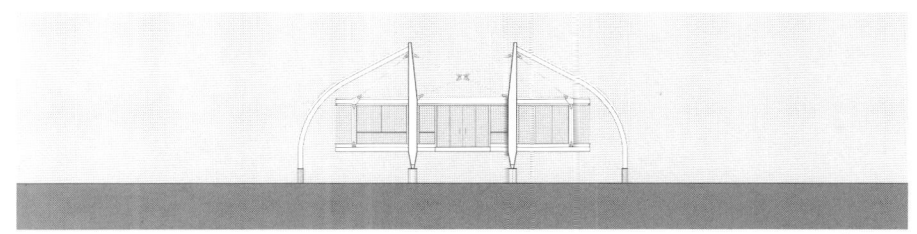

Elevation

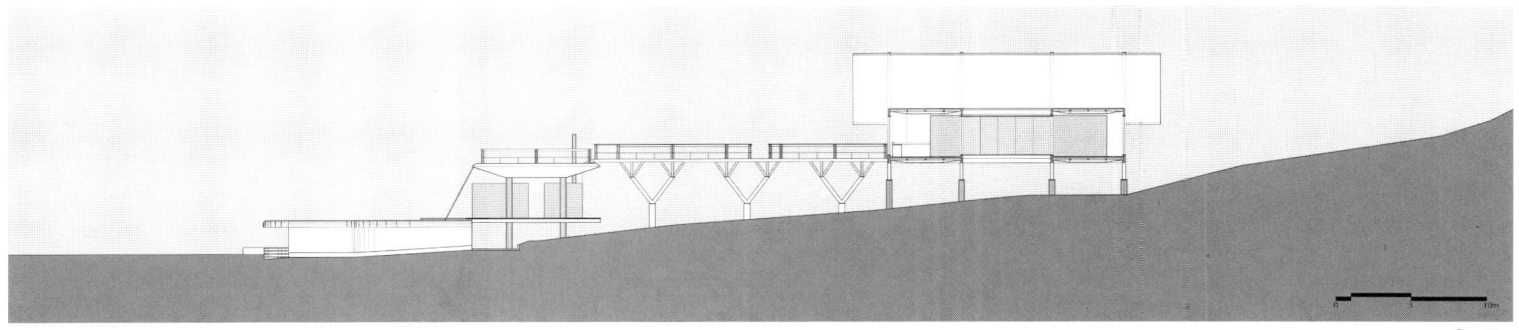

Section

Living room　居間

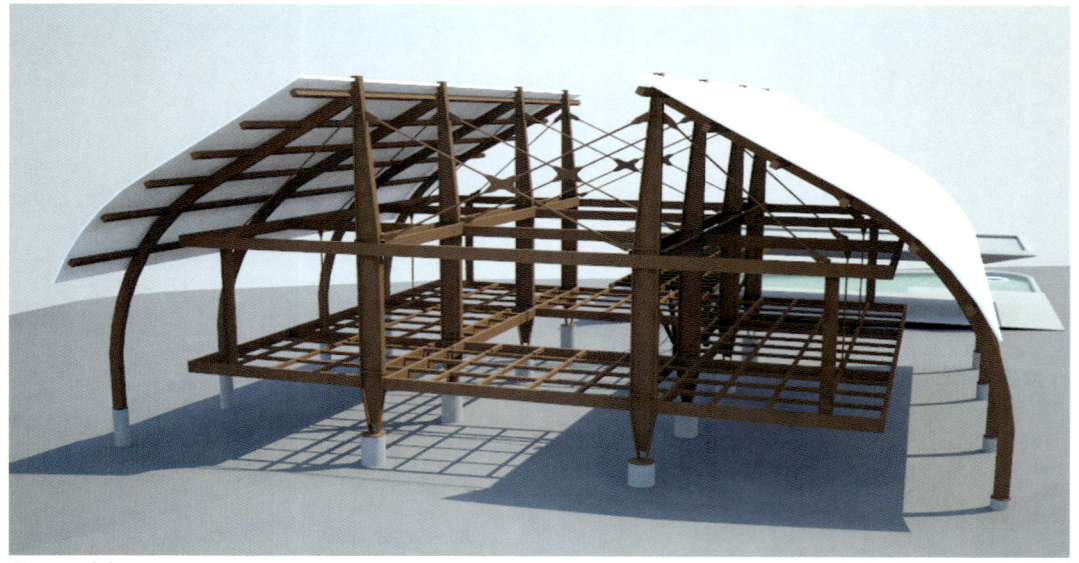

Structural diagram

Corridor 廊下△▽

Architects: GESTO Ambiental–arquitetura e urbanismo—Newton Massafumi Yamato and Tânia Regina Parma, principals-in-charge; Wilson Pombeiro, project team
Clients: Miss and Mr. Spagnuollo
Consultants: Yopanan Rebello, structural
Program: weekend house
Structural system: steel
Major materials: steel, wood, glass and natural fiber (roof)
Site area: 5,000 m²
Built area: 420 m²
Total floor area: 840 m² (including outside spaces)

View with curved roof　湾曲する屋根越しの風景

Corner: kitchen on right　角部：右は台所

View toward bathroom 浴室方向を見る

Courtyard 中庭

Living room 居間

PROCTER-RIHL ARCHITECTS

SLICE HOUSE

Porto Alegre, RS, Brazil
Design: 2002– Construction: –2004

Photos: Yoshio F.

The project was selected to represent Brazil in the IV Latin American Architecture Biennale in October 2004 in Peru. The house makes a series of references to Brazilian modern architecture as well as adding a new element with its complex prismatic geometry, which generates a series of spatial illusions in the interior spaces.

Brownfield Sites—Residual Sites put back into the Urban Matrix
The changing nature of the urban context generates through time a number of odd residual sites. Procter-Rihl has a special interest in residual urban sites and believes urban centres should be developed to maximum potential, as no site is too small or unimportant to be left aside. Residual sites can be extremely interesting because they impose difficult questions to solve in terms of planning and programme. They are definitely rich areas to explore. This project is placed on a site 3.7 m wide x 38.5 m long. It is located in a good neighbourhood of Porto Alegre (Brazil) but has been vacant for more than 20 years. It went to auction 3 times during this long period without any interest whatsoever. The client was the only one to put in an offer on the 4th auction, as people could not see the potential.

Client and Neighbourhood
The client, a 65 years old History lecturer, gave Procter-Rihl a brief to design a space for entertaining with understated materials but extravagant in its spatial solutions. She had previous experience with renovations so the building process was not completely new. Originally, the client gave a brief for a one bedroom house which was adjusted to 2 bedrooms, open plan living dining space, a private garden living space, main bedroom with ensuite bath and generous walk-in dressing closet, and 1 or 2 garage spaces. Light was important with the emphasis on natural daylight with solar control and ventilation in order to minimise the need for air conditioning. She believed architecture could suggest different ways of living and was up for the challenge. In terms of budget, she preferred to spend money on interesting spaces rather than expensive finishes. She was very committed to generate a piece of architecture, rather than an ordinary building and realised collaboration between client and architect was essential. The cost of the building per square meter was slightly less than an average middle class construction.

The conservative neighbourhood was not immediately taken by the project. The Brazilian middle class had become much more conservative in terms of architectural taste. Postmodernism is the developers' architectural language and is very much what people expect. Architecture is not part of the media debate unlike in Europe, which has made architectural discourse very insular in Latin America. Procter-Rihl believes good architecture should have a role in questioning values in society and engaging architectural debate. The development of the exterior garden and final louvre grill details changed the neighbourhood perception of the house as it completed the original vision. The selection to represent Brazil in the Ibero-Latin American Arch Biennale helped to validate the project. The house stills attracts curiosity from all over but is now fairly accepted by the neighbourhood.

Multi-Cultural Identity—Hybrid of Brazilian and British Culture
The project is a hybrid of Brazilian and British concerns. Although the building makes reference to Brazilian modernist architecture, its form takes a more contemporary European interest in asymmetrical complexity. Brazilian elements are the implementation of local concrete engineering, open plan typology, large extrovert spaces, swimming pool, outdoor living and lush garden flora. Concrete is not used in a typical Brazilian grand engineering gesture or sculptural form, but something more discrete. Thin continuous reinforced concrete structural walls bridge over the long slot windows and garage bay, but are not expressed as beams and disappear within the skin of the building. The diagonal concrete stair beam, which angles down to support the cantilevered corridor also disappears into a wrapping ribbon line, which flows around the courtyard.

Brazilian rawness comes through using materials such as timber formed poured concrete whereas British precision is a by-product of modular steel component construction. The building skin reflects these two halves. The steel front facade cladding, roof, gutters and grillwork is all detailed in a British way. Other British elements are the structural glass of the pool, attention to detailing and the use of Brazilian plants in a less formal natural layering common to British landscaping.

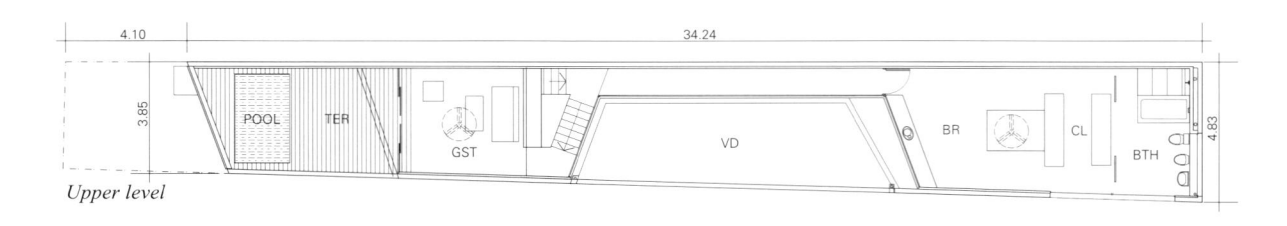

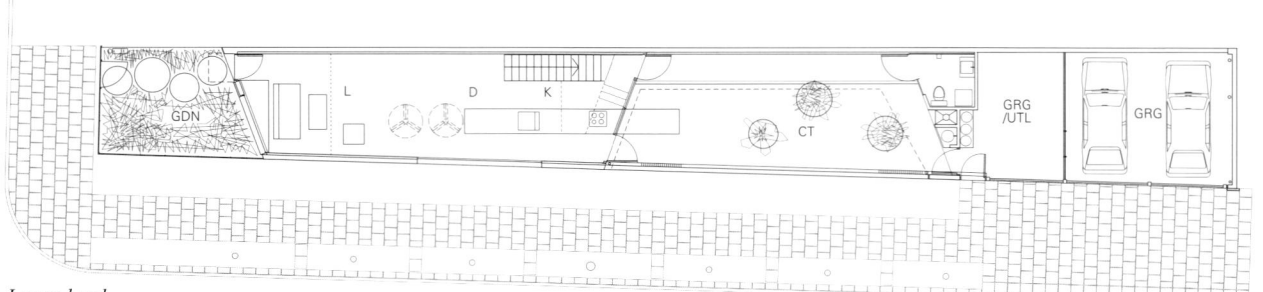

Upper level

Lower level

このプロジェクトは，ペルーで開催された2004年，10月の第4回ラテンアメリカ建築ビエンナーレのブラジル代表作品として選ばれたものである。この住宅では，その内部に一連の空間的幻影を生み出す，複雑で，プリズムのような幾何学形態による新しいエレメントを加えると同時に，ブラジル現代建築への一連の参照を行っている。

〈ブラウンフィールド・サイト――都市のマトリックスに戻された残余の敷地〉

変化する都市のコンテクストは，常時，数多くの意外な残余の敷地を発生させる。私たちは余白として残されたままの都市の敷地に特別な関心があり，都市の中心部はその可能性を最大限まで開発すべきであり，考慮の余地のない，小さすぎたり，つまらない敷地はないと信じている。残余の敷地は，プランニングやプログラムの点で解決の難しい問題を提起するがゆえに，非常に面白いものに成り得る。そこは探求するに断然豊かな領域である。このプロジェクトの敷地は幅3.7メートル，長さ38.5メートル。ポルト・アレグレの申し分のない優良地区にあるが，20年以上も空き地のままであった。この長い期間に3回，オークションにかけられたが，何の関心も惹かなかった。誰もその土地の可能性を理解できなかったので，クライアントは4回目のオークションで指し値をつけた唯一の人物であった。

〈クライアントと近隣住民〉

クライアントである65歳の歴史家は，私たちに，材料は地味だが空間構成に於いては贅沢な，人を楽しませてくれる空間をデザインするための概要を提示した。彼女は以前にも改築の経験があり，建築のプロセスについて全く知らないわけではない。当初の要望は，2寝室にも調整できる1寝室住宅で，オープン・プランのリビング・ダイニング，プライベート・ガーデンとなる生活空間，浴室と広いウォークイン・クローゼットが付いた主寝室，1～2台収容できるガレージであった。光は大切で，空調の必要を最小限にするために陽射しの制御と自然換気と共に自然光を重視した。彼女は，建築は異なる生活の仕方を示唆し，チャレンジの可能性を提供できるものと信じていた。費用の点では，贅沢な仕上げよりも面白い空間をつくることの方にお金をかけることを良しとしている。彼女は普通の建物というよりは建築作品を生み出すことに強くこだわり，クライアントと建築家の間の協力を実現することが不可欠であった。平米あたりの工費は中級レベルの標準よりわずかに少ない。

保守的な近隣住民は，このプロジェクトをすぐには認めなかった。ブラジルの中産階級は建築の好みについてかなり保守的になっている。ポストモダニズムは開発業者の建築言語であり，人々がまさに期待するものだ。建築はヨーロッパとは違ってメディアの論争の一部ではなく，ラテンアメリカでの建築的な論考を孤立的なものにしている。屋外庭園の展開とルーバー格子のディテールは最終的に，最初の構想をそのまま完成させつつ，近隣住民のこの家に対する見解を変えさせることになった。イベロ＝ラテン・アメリカ建築ビエンナーレのブラジル代表に選ばれたことが，このプロジェクトの正当性を立証するのを助けてくれた。この家は依然としてそこらじゅうからの好奇心を引きつけているが，今では近隣住民によってまずまず受け入れられている。

〈多文化的個性――ブラジルと英国の文化〉

このプロジェクトはブラジルと英国に関わる事柄の混成物である。ブラジリアン・モダニストの建築を参照しているが，その形態はより今日的なヨーロッパの関心である非対称的な複雑性を帯びている。ブラジル的エレメントは，地元のコンクリート技術との関係，オープン・プランの建築類型，外向的な広い空間，スイミング・プール，戸外のリビング，庭の豊かな植生である。コンクリートは，ブラジルでは典型的な，大げさな技術的ジェスチャーや彫刻的形態をとらず，それらとはいくぶん分離されたものとなっている。この鉄筋コンクリートの連続する薄い構造壁は，細長くとられた窓とガレージの区画を架け渡しているが，梁として表現されず，建物の皮膜の中に消えている。片持ちとなった廊下を支持するために下に角度を向けた，コンクリート造の斜めに進む階段梁もまたコートヤードの周りを流れて包み込む，リボン状のラインの中に消えて行く。

ブラジル的なラフさは木造型枠の現場打ちコンクリートのような材料の使い方を通して現れる一方，英国的な緻密さは規格単位で構成されたスティール部材による建設の副産物である。建物の外皮には，これら2つが半々に反映されている。スティールの正面被覆，屋根，樋，格子のディテールはすべて英国式である。その他の英国的エレメントには，プールの構造ガラス，細部構成への注意の集中，英国の景観構成に広く行き渡っている形式張らない自然な重ね方でブラジルの植物を扱っていることがあげられる。

View from approach アプローチより見る

Living/dining room: view toward courtyard　居間／食堂：中庭方向を見る

Living room: pool above 居間：上部に見えるのはプール

View toward guest room over terrace and pool テラス／プール越しにゲストルームを見る

Architects: Procter-Rihl Architects—
Fernando Rihl and Christopher Procter, principals-in-charge; Dirk Anderson, James Backwell, Johannes Lobbert, project team
Client: Neusa Oliveira
Consultants: Michael Baigent, MBOK (glass and steel), Antonio Pasquali (concrete), structural; Vitor Pasin, foundation; Flavio Mainardi, services engineer; Mauro Medeiros, site architect
General contractor: J. S. Construction
Structural system: reinforced concrete
Major materials: concrete
Site area: 240 m²
Building area: 80 m²
Total floor area: 240 m²

Upper level: view toward courtyard from bedroom 上階：寝室より中庭を見る

View from guest room toward terrace ゲストルームよりテラスを見る

Courtyard with natural light faces kitchen, living/dining room　自然光が差し込む中庭：台所，居間／食堂に面する

Downward view of courtyard　中庭見下ろし

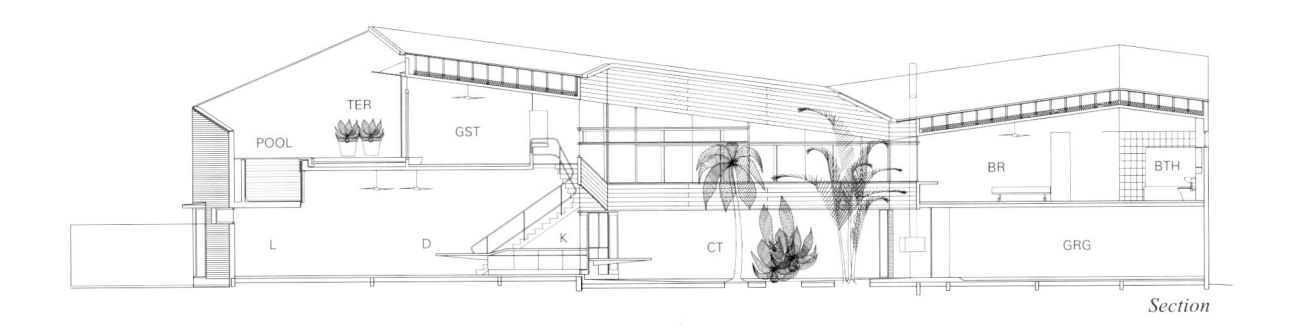

Section

View from corridor on upper level. Courtyard on left 上階の廊下より見る。左に中庭

Staircase leading to upper level (left). Kitchen counter and dining table (right)
上階へつづく階段（左）。キッチンカウンターとダイニングテーブル（右）

View from upper part of staircase: bedroom above and living/dining room below
階段上部より見る：上に寝室，下に居間／食堂

View from guest room: courtyard (left) and corridor (right)　ゲスト・ルームより見る：中庭（左）と廊下（右）

MARCOS ACAYABA

MILAN HOUSE

São Paulo, SP, Brazil
Design: 1972–73 Construction: 1973–75

Photos: Yoshio F.

Milan House was constructed in a site of great dimensions with squared proportions and in a mild slope. As in relation to the site, the construction area would not be too big, a lot of space for the garden was left.

Considering the well balanced proportion between the construction and the open space allowed by the generous site's dimension, the design's assumption was to enhance the relationship between the house and the garden.

The solution was to create a reinforced concrete shell, like a vault, which rests in four points on its vertices. This shell is conceived as a roof which shelters huge inner open spaces, visually connected to the tropical garden surrounding the house. A linear slab placed under the vault combines three different half levels organizing the house's program.

The peculiarly designed space is defined by the contrast between the light shell, the linear slab and the site in half levels. The flow between the inner and outer space is continuous and multiple, avoiding repetitive paths, and dead-ends. The transparence is the main characteristic of the project.

The bedrooms, on the upper level, are closed only by wooden sliding doors and ventilation flaps, which integrate them to the interior space. Internally the house is completely open with exception to the bathrooms, which are located in two towers that concentrate the hydraulic installations with water reservoirs on top. The lavatories as situated outside the bathrooms and integrated in the inner terrace located in front of the bedrooms. The living room is circumscribed by three glazed walls, and a volume with a fireplace between a sofa and book-shelf.

The intermediate slab is stretched over the pilotis area outlining a solarium and reaches on the opposite side the site's highest level. Finally, the red cement tiled floor unifies the inside and outside areas.

ミラン邸は緩やかに傾斜する方形の広い敷地に建てられている。敷地の大きさに対して建築面積は広すぎるというほどではなく、庭園として使える土地がたっぷりと残された。

敷地の広大さからもたらされる豊かなオープンスペースと建物との均整を上手くとろうと考えると、デザインの前提として、住宅と庭園との関係を強調する必要がある。

ヴォールトのように4つの頂点に支えられた鉄筋コンクリートのシェルをつくりだすことが答えになった。シェルは、周囲のトロピカル・ガーデンと視覚的に結ばれた広大なオープンスペースを覆う屋根とみなされている。ヴォールトの下に据えられたリニアなスラブが、住宅の諸室を編成する半階づつ異なる3つのレベルを結びつける。

一風変わったデザインで構成された空間は、軽快なシェル、半階づつ異なるリニアなスラブおよび敷地との対比によって決定づけられている。内部と外部の空間の流れは、径路の反復や行き止まりを避け、連続的で多彩である。透明性がこのプロジェクトの主要な特徴となっている。

上階の寝室は、木の引き戸と換気用フラップによってのみ閉ざされ、開けば内部空間に統合される。内部空間は、頂部に貯水槽を載せた給水設備が集まる2つのタワー内に位置する浴室を除いて完全にオープンな構成である。洗面所は浴室の外に配され、寝室の前にある内部テラスと一体化する。居間は3面をガラス壁に、残る面はソファと書棚、そのあいだに挟まれた暖炉に囲まれている。

中間に位置するスラブがピロティ・エリアを越えて延び、ソラリウムの輪郭を描き、敷地の最高部である反対側まで達する。そして最後に、赤いセメントタイルを貼り詰めた床が内部と外部を一体化する。

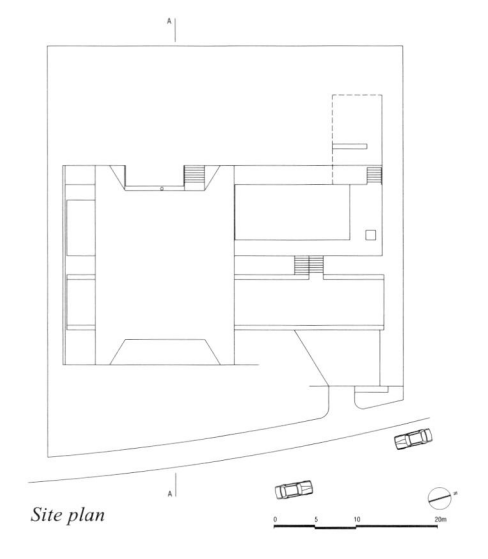

Site plan

Lower level

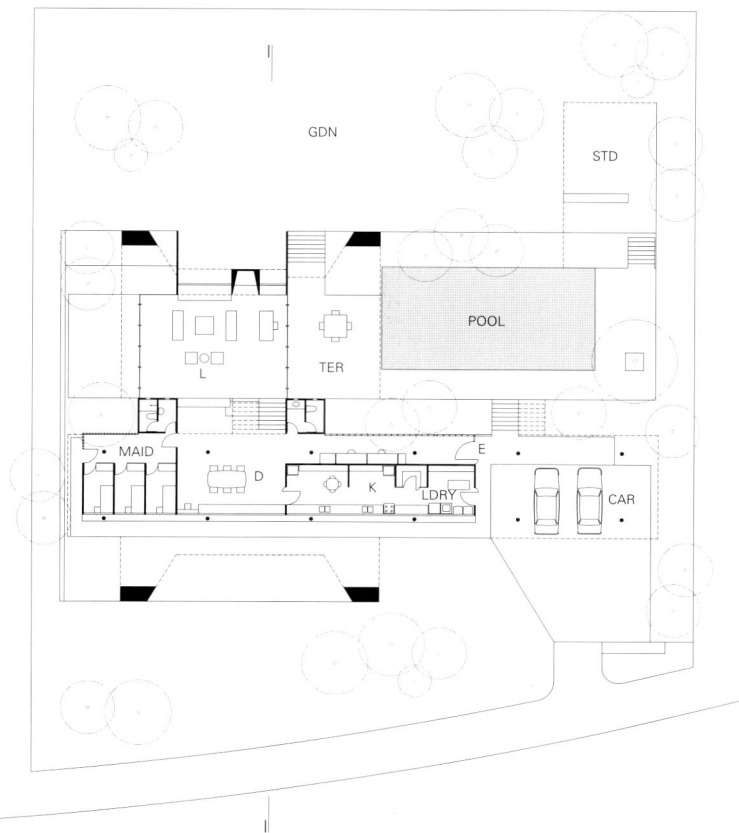

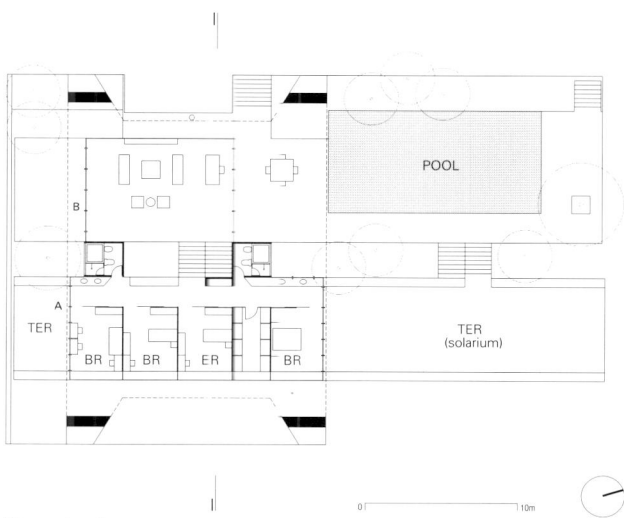

Upper level

Architects: Marcos Acayaba Arquitetos—
Marcos Acayaba, principal-in-charge;
Marlene Milan Acayaba, project team
Client: Betty Milan
Consultants: Ugo Tedeschi and Yukio Ogata, structural; Antonio Garcia Martinez and Olavo Mota, mechanical
General contractor: CENPLA
Structural system: reiforced concrete, shell, slab
Major materials: natural exposed concrete, painted exposed concrete, stone masonry walls
Site area: 2,150 m^2
Building area 467 m^2
Total floor area: 791 m^2 (interior area, 361 m^2 + terraces and carport, 430 m^2)

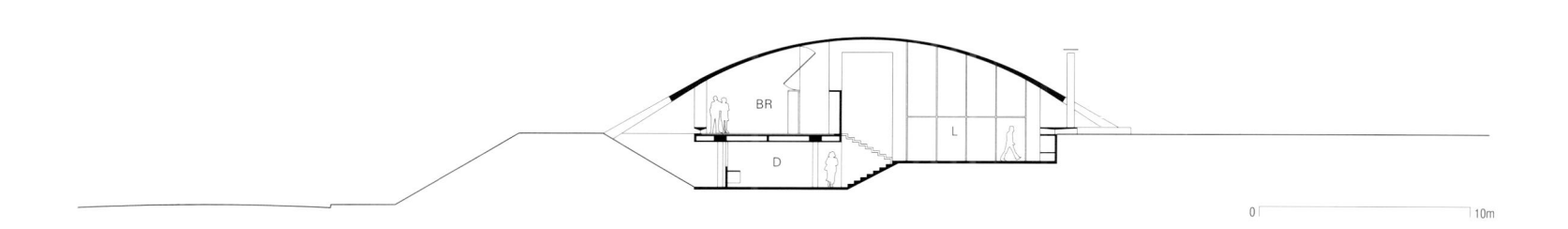

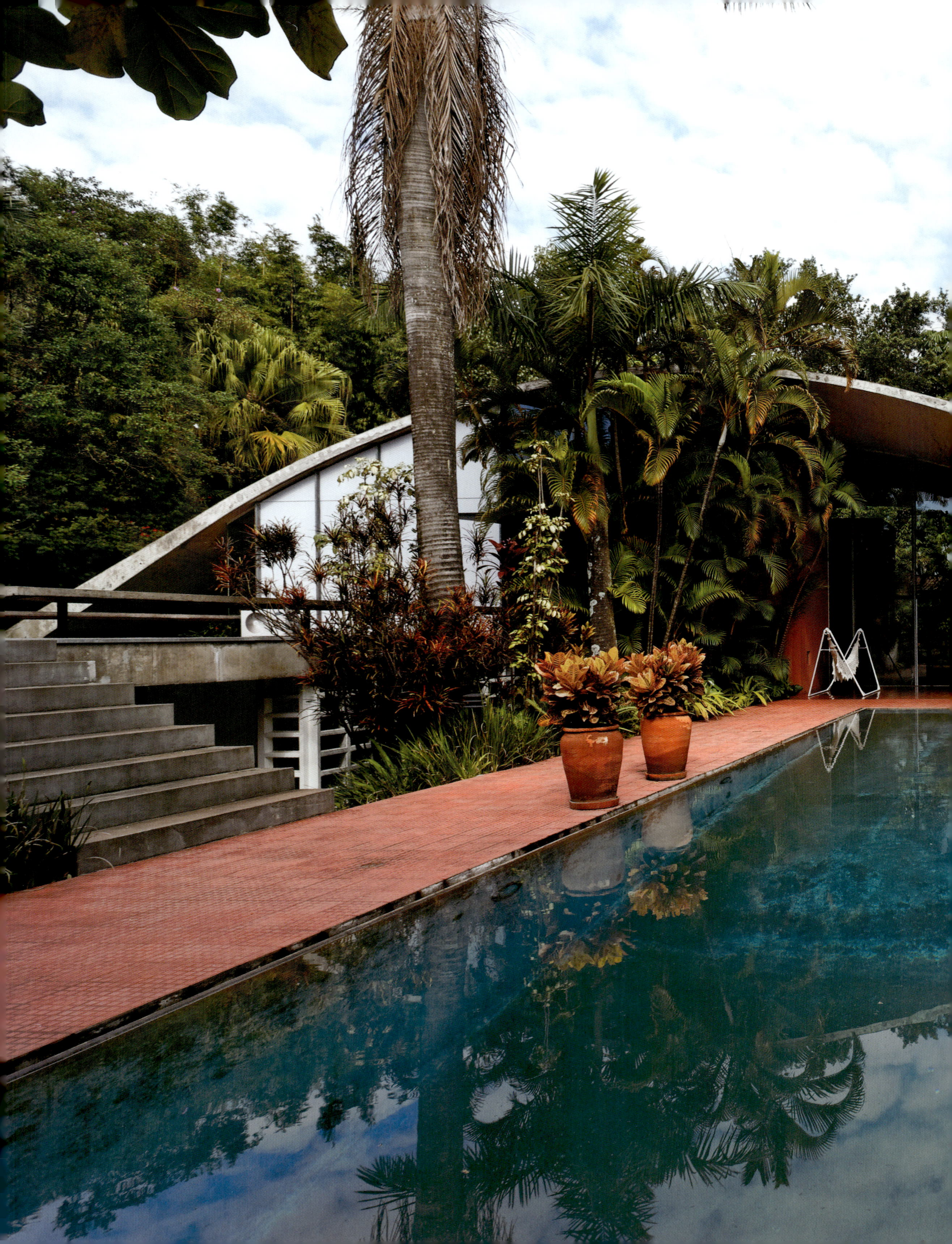

Overall view from pool　プール越しに見る全景

View toward entrance: carport on left　玄関方向を見る。左はガレージ

South terrace on upper level　上階南側テラス

View from carport: staircase leading to pool　ガレージより見る：階段の先にプールがある

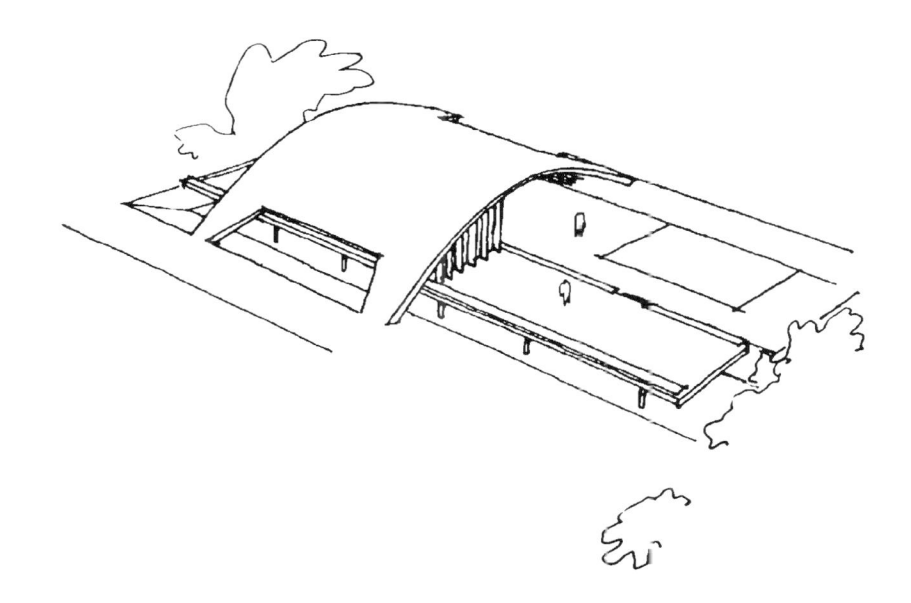

Pass under eaves: entrance to kitchen on right　軒裏の通路：右は台所への入口

133

South terrace on lower level　下階南側テラス

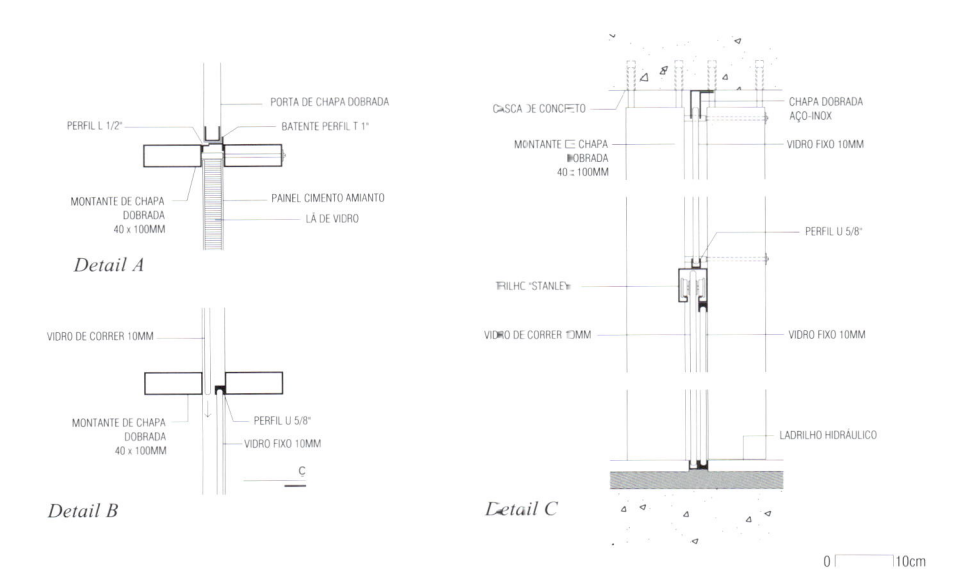

South terrace: concrete vault-like shell covering whole space　南側テラス：ヴォールト状のコンクリート・シェルが全体を覆う

Detail A

Detail B

Detail C

0 — 10cm

View toward terrace from garden　庭よりテラスを見る

Entrance 玄関

View of living room from terrace on south　南側のテラスより居間を見る

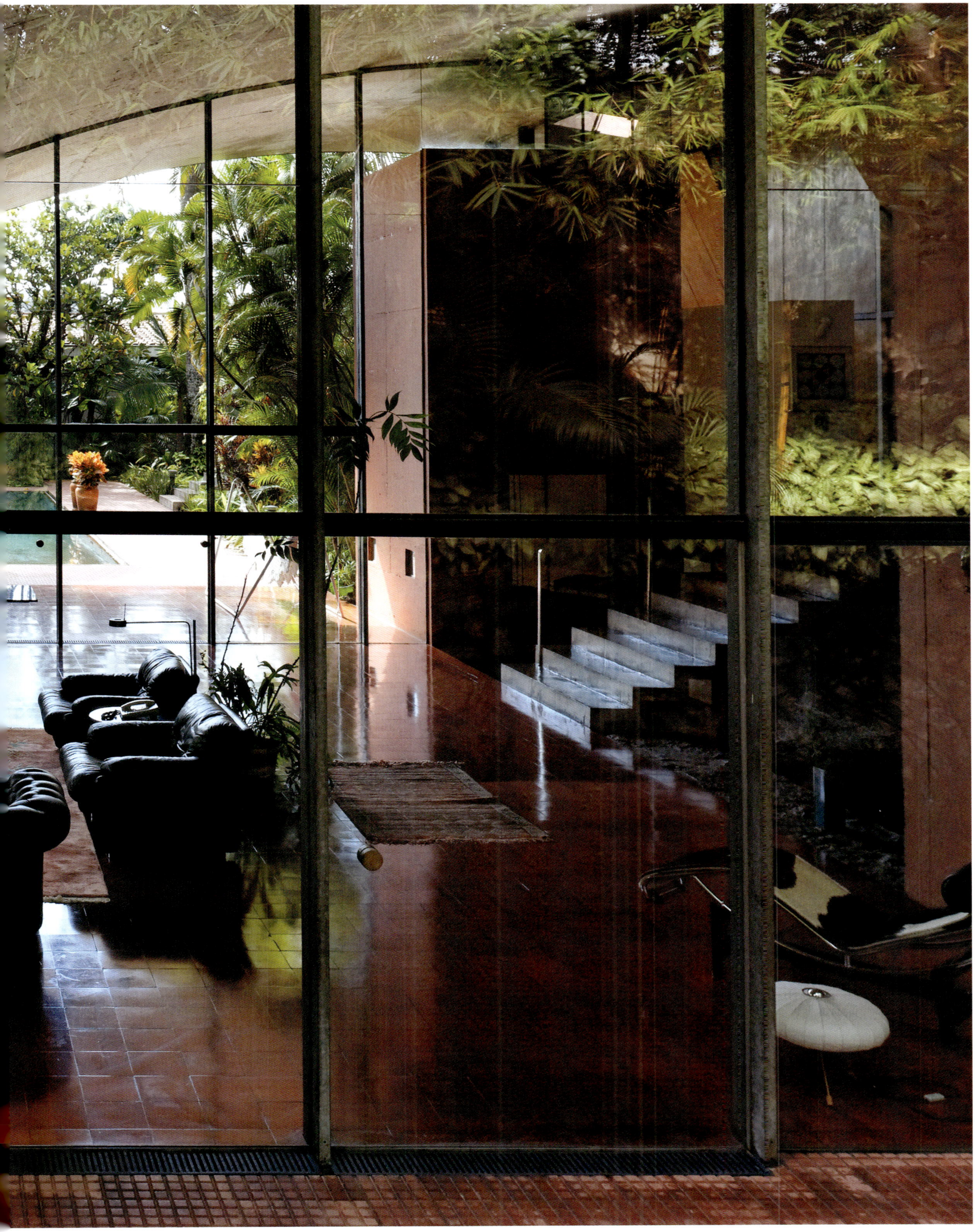

Living room　居間

Terrace: pool on right, living room on left. Staircase leading to garden　テラス：右はプール，左は居間。階段の先は庭

Staircase of living room: bedrooms above, dining room below　居間の階段：上は寝室，下は食堂

Living room　居間

Living room　居間

Living room is on mezzanine between bedrooms above and dining room below　居間は上階寝室と下階ダイニングの間にある

Dining room 食堂

View from dining room toward living room 食堂より居間を見る

△▽Dining room　食堂

Opening of dining room 食堂の開口部

Corridor: bedroom on right, pivoting wooden flap for ventilation above 廊下：右の寝室上部には通風用の回転式木製扉がある

Bedroom 寝室

SOU FUJIMOTO

HOUSE N

Oita, Japan
Design: 2006–07 Construction: 2007–08

Photos: Yoshio F.

Overall view 全景

A home for two plus a dog. The house itself is comprised of three shells of progressive size nested inside one another. The outermost shell covers the entire premises, creating a covered, semi-indoor garden. Second shell encloses a limited space inside the covered outdoor space. Third shell is a small house within a house.

I have always had doubts about a house being separated from the streets by a single wall, and wondered that a rich gradation of domain defined by various distances between streets and houses might be a possibility, such as: a place inside the house that is fairly near the street; a place that is a bit far from the street; and a place far off the street, in secure privacy.

That is why life in this house resembles to living among the clouds. A distinct boundary is nowhere to be found, but spaces generated by faint shades of relationships. One might say that an ideal architecture is an outdoor space that feels like the indoors and an indoor space that feels like the outdoors. In a nested structure, the inside is invariably the outside, and vice versa. It is not about space nor about form, but simply about expressing the riches of what are 'between' the house and the streets.

Three nested shells eventually mean infinite nesting because the whole world is made up of infinite nesting. And here are only three of them that are given barely visible shape. I imagined that the city and the house are no different from one another, but different expressions of the same thing—an undulation of a primordial space for human dwelling. This is a presentation of a house in which everything from the origins of the world to a specific house is conceived together under a single method.
Sou Fujimoto

家族2人と犬のための3重入れ子の住宅。一番外側の殻は敷地全体を覆っており，半ば室内のように覆われた庭をつくり出す。2番目の殻はその囲まれた外部空間の中にさらに限定された場所を囲いとる。3番目の殻は，家の中の小さな家である。

街と家とが，壁一枚で隔てられているということに疑問を感じていた。むしろ，家だけれどもだいぶ街に近い場所，街から少し遠ざかった場所，街からすごく遠くなって，プライバシーも守られた場所，のように，街と家とのあいだには，幾つもの距離感を伴った豊かな領域のグラデーションがありえるのではないだろうか。

この住宅は，雲の中に住むことに似ている。どこまで行っても明確な境界が存在せず，かすかな関係の濃淡によって場が生まれる。理想の建築とは，内部のような外部空間であり，外部のような内部空間であると言えるのではないだろうか。そして入れ子においては，内部は常に外部であり，外部は常に内部である。空間ではなく，形態ではなく，ただ，家と街との「あいだ」の豊かさを顕在化する。

3重の入れ子とは，つまり無限の入れ子である。世界が無限の入れ子でできていて，その間のほんの3つが，かすかに目に見える形を与えられている。都市と住宅とは，けっして別々のものではなく，人が住むための根源的な空間の起伏の濃淡という意味で，同じものの違った現れである。世界の成り立ちから一軒の家までを，一つの方法によって同時に構想した住宅の提案。　　　　　　　　（藤本壮介）

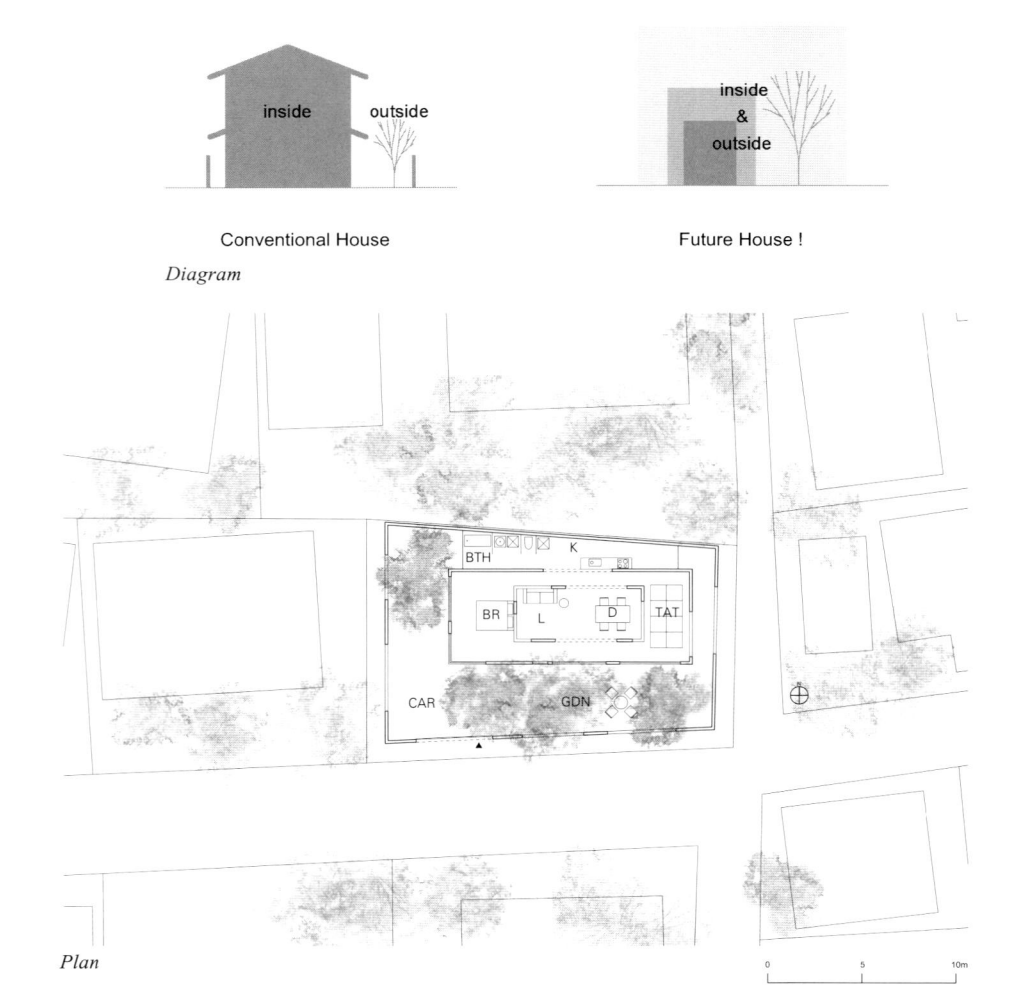

Site plan

Diagram

Conventional House　　　　Future House !

Plan

Architects: Sou Fujimoto Architects—
Sou Fujimoto, principal-in-charge;
Yumiko Nogiri, project team
Consultants: Jun Sato Structural Engineers—
Jun Sato, structural; Sirius Lighting Office—
Hirohito Totsune, lighting
General contractor: Saiki Kensetsu
Structural system: reinforced concrete
Major materials: reinforced concrete, glass, wood, exterior and interior
Site area: 236.57 m^2
Built area: 150.57 m^2
Total floor area: 85.51 m^2

South elevation: entrance and parking on left 南面：左に玄関と車庫入口

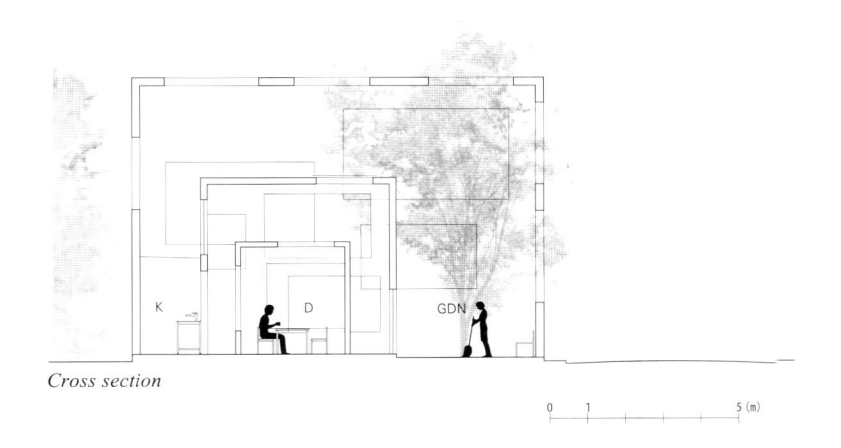

Cross section

0 1 5 (m)

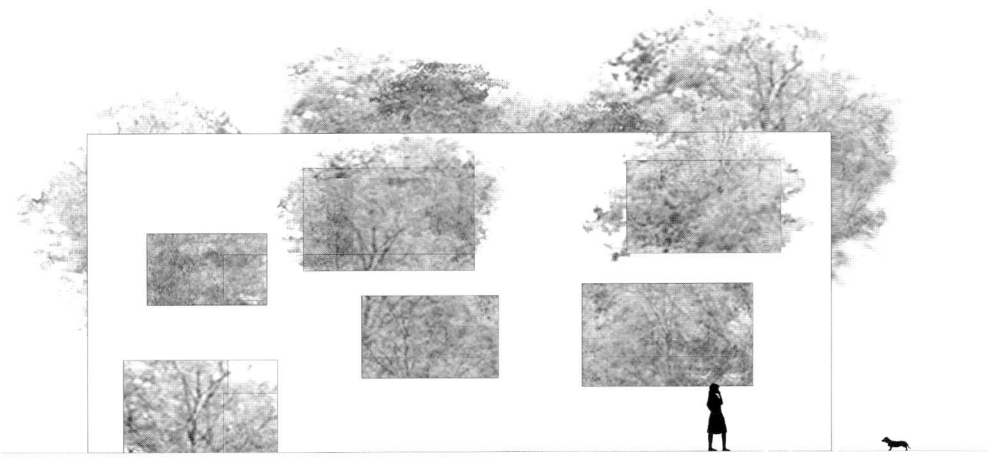

South elevation

149

△▷ *Evening view: south elevation*　夕景：南面

151

Garden 庭

Void over roof (left) and garden (right): looking east　屋根（左）と庭（右）上部のヴォイド：東を見る

View from entrance toward garden　玄関より庭を見る

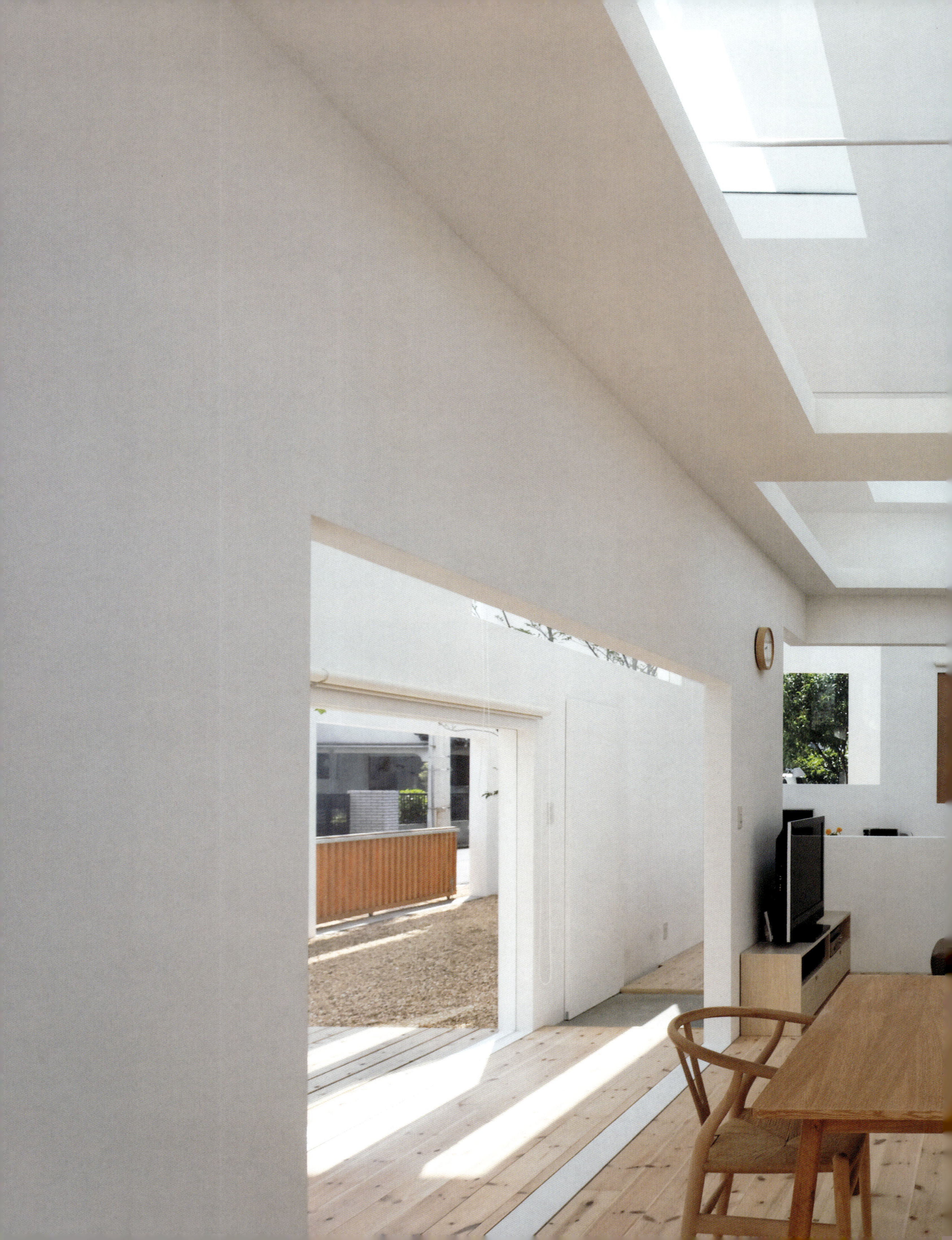

Dining/living room: kitchen on right, garden on left　食堂／居間：右に台所，左に庭

Dining room 食堂

View toward garden from dining/living room 食堂／居間より庭を見る

Tatami room: looking dining room through holes on wall　和室：壁に開けられた穴越しに食堂を見る

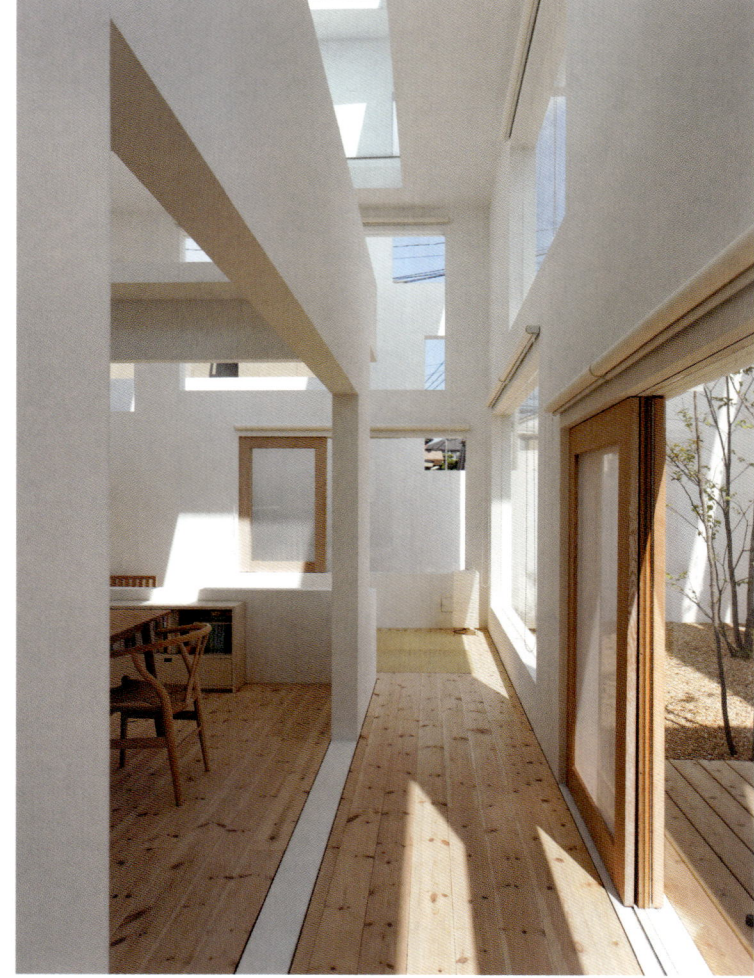

Downward view of study and bedroom　書斎／寝室見下ろし

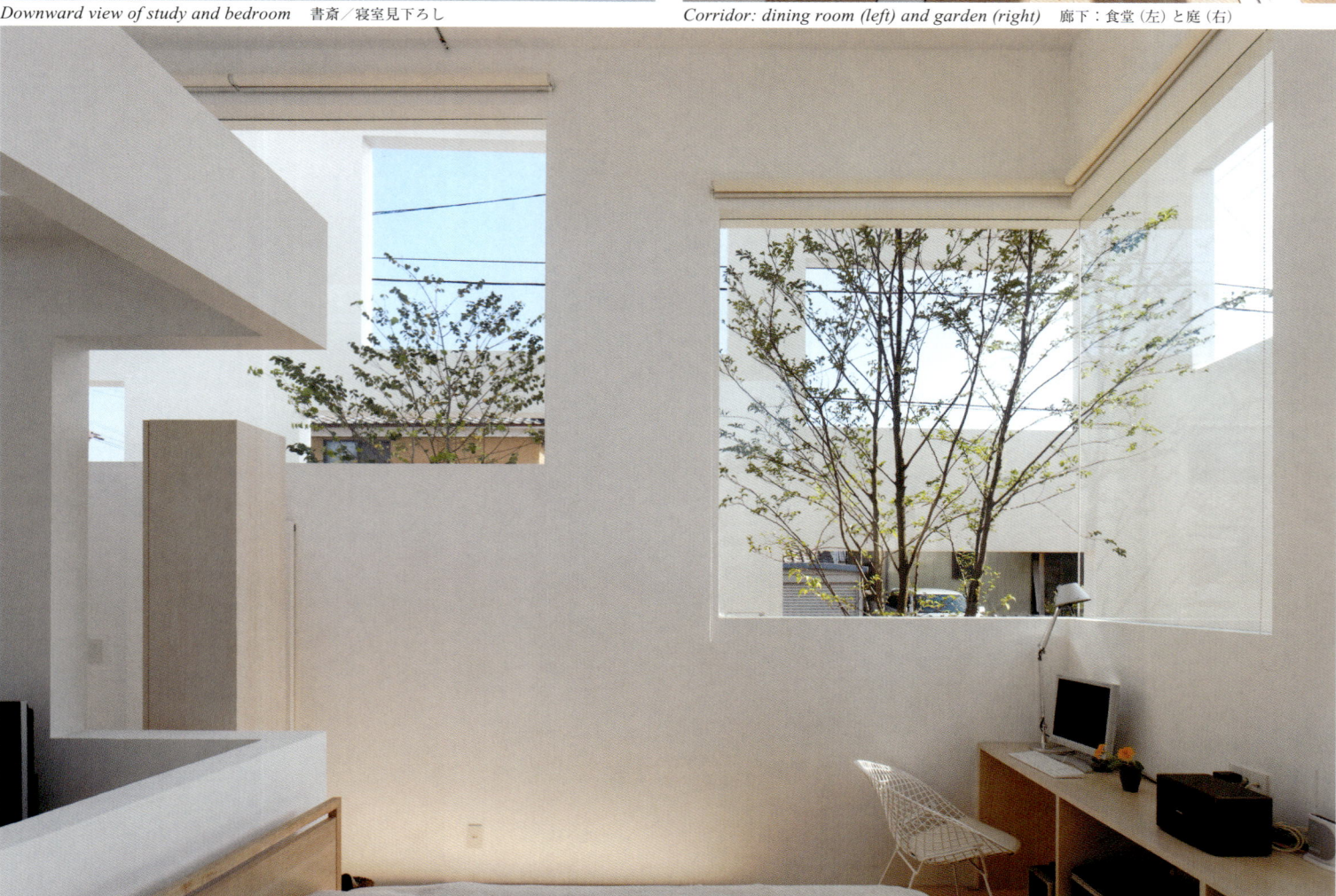

Corridor: dining room (left) and garden (right)　廊下：食堂（左）と庭（右）

Bedroom/study: looking south　寝室／書斎：南を見る

View from bedroom　寝室より見る

SOU FUJIMOTO

FINAL WOODEN HOUSE
Kumamoto, Japan
Design: 2005–06 Construction: 2007–08

Photos: Yoshio F.

In this project, I intended to produce an ultimate building produced in timber material. The method is to solely pile up cedar timber material in 350 mm x 350 mm. In the end, an archetypical scene, which is premature to be called as an architecture could emerge.

Wood has an extremely all-round capability as a building material. In that very sense, wood materials are handily adapted in various parts and points in typical wooden buildings—from columns and beams, foundation, exterior and interior walls, ceiling and flooring, to insulation, furniture, stairs, window frames—which means everything. However, if the wooden material has such all-round capability, in that very sense it is possible to produce an architecture by applying this all-round material as "a single operation method"; in other words, a new kind of space will be created where everything is blended and integrated as one; it is remained as the state before the differentiation and specialization of those particular functionalities of a building has occurred—before the definition of a building such as columns or beams fix the role of each part within a building.

There is no differentiation as a floor, a wall, and a ceiling in this building. The part recognized as a floor would be a chair or a ceiling or a wall from other view points. The floor levels are in relative conditions so that a space can appear differently according to the location of the occupant. Occupants will be distributed three-dimensionally within a space, and the distances between occupants will be recognized as a new kind of sensation and notion—the space will be as if like a topography without the differentiation and the specialization of a typical building. The occupant will find out various functionalities within this rise and fall of the space.

Isn't it possible to say that this bungalow no longer fits within the category of a wooden architecture? If an architecture produced by timber material is defined as wooden architecture, in this project the application and utilization of timber material goes beyond the common architectural procedure, which is more directly connected with "the place where people occupies". It is the archetypical existence, while it is too primitive to be called as an architecture; it is rather a new formation and a new kind of existence, than to be called as a new kind of architecture.
Sou Fujimoto

究極の木造建築を作ることを考えた。350mm角の杉材を，ただひたすら積んでいく。その先に建築以前の原型的な場所が立ち現れてくる。

木材というものは恐ろしく万能である。そして通常の木造建築では，木材はその万能性ゆえにさまざまな場所に器用に使い分けられる。柱や梁，下地材，外壁，内壁，天井，床材，断熱材，家具，階段，窓枠，つまりすべてである。しかし万能であるのなら，逆にただ一つの方法によって，これら全てを満たすような建築を作ることができるのではないだろうか。さまざまな機能や役割が細分化する以前の，渾然一体となった未分化の状態を保持した新しい空間を創り出す。

ここには床，壁，天井といった区別はない。床だと思っていたところが，別の場所から見ると椅子であり天井であり壁である。床レベルは相対的であり，人が居る場所によって空間が違って見えてくる。人が空間の中に立体的に分布する。それは新しい距離感として体験される未分化の地形のような場所である。住み手はこの起伏の中に，さまざまな機能を見出していく。

このバンガローは，もはや木造建築という範疇には納まらないのではないだろうか。木で作られた建築が木造建築であるとすれば，このバンガローでは，木そのものが建築的な手続きを飛び越えて「人の居る場所」にダイレクトにつながっている。建築以前といってもいい原初的な存在である。それは新しい建築であるというよりも，新しい成り立ちであり，新しい存在である。

（藤本壮介）

Under construction   *: Sou Fujimoto Architects

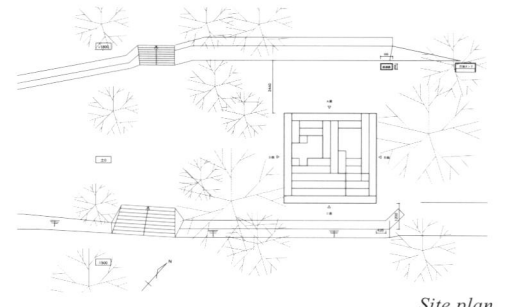

Site plan

Distant view over river 川越しに見る遠景

Bungalow made of rectangular wood pieces entirely　角材を積み上げて形づくられたヴォリューム

Detail: exterior wall with openings　ディテール：開口部のある外壁

Interior with natural light through various openings　開口部から自然光が差し込む内部

165

Architects: Sou Fujimoto Architects—
Sou Fujimoto, principal-in-charge;
Hiroshi Kato, project team
Clients: Kumamura Forestry Association
Consultants: Jun Sato Structural Engineers—
Jun Sato, Naotake Koyama, structural; Sirius
Lighting Office—Hirohito Totsune, lighting
General contractor: Tanakagumi Construction—
Toshihiko Shiraki
Structural system: wood
Major materials: wood, exterior and interior
Site area: 89.30 m^2
Built area: 15.13 m^2
Total floor area: 15.13 m^2 (except loft, 7.5 m^2)

Various seans of interior space　様々なシーンが展開する内部

Sectional detail S=1:75

Level Y00-Y04

Level Y05-Y10 S=1:100

Elevation A S=1:100

Elevation B

Elevation C

Elevation D

GA DOCUMENT
Global Architecture

GA DOCUMENT presents the finest in international design, focusing on architecture that expresses our times and striving to record the history of contemporary architecture. Striking black-and-white and vibrant color photographs presented in a generous format make for a dynamic re-presentation of spaces, materials and textures. International scholars and critics provide insightful texts to further inform the reader of the most up-to-date ideas and events in the profession.

多様に広がり、変化を見せる世界の現代建築の動向をデザインの問題を中心に取り上げ、現代建築の完全な記録をめざしつつ、時代の流れに柔軟に対応した独自の視点から作品をセレクションし、新鮮な情報を世界に向けて発信する唯一のグローバルな建築専門誌。掲載する作品をすべて現地取材、撮影することで大型誌面にダイナミックに表現し、その空間、ディテールやテクスチャーを的確に再現する。

Japanese and English text, Size: 300 × 297mm

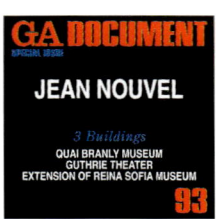

93 SPECIAL ISSUE: JEAN NOUVEL
インタヴュー：「近況、そして3つの建物について」ジャン・ヌヴェル
作品：ケ・ブランリー美術館／ガスリー劇場／レイナ・ソフィア国立中央美術館増築棟
Interview: "Recent and Three Buildings" Jean Nouvel
Works: Quai Branly Museum; Guthrie Theater; Extension of National Center Museum of Reina Sofia

132 pages, 114 in color ¥2,848

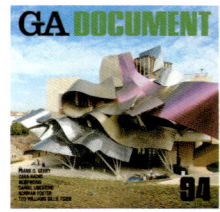

94
作品：F・O・ゲーリー ホテル・マルケス・デ・リスカル／Z・ハディド R・ロペス・デ・エレディア・ヴィナ・トンドニア／モーフォシス NOAA衛星センター／N・フォスター ハースト・タワー／D・リベスキンド デンバー美術館ハミルトン・ビルディング／他
プロジェクト：F・O・ゲーリー／Z・ハディド／モーフォシス
Works: F. O. Gehry Hotel at Marques de Riscal; Z. Hadid R. Lopez De Heredia Viña Tondonia; Morphosis NOAA Satellite Operations Facility; N. Foster Hearst Tower; T. Williams B. Tsien Phoenix Art Museum Expansion; and others
Projects: F. O. Gehry; Z. Hadid; Morphosis

108 pages, 66 in color ¥2,848

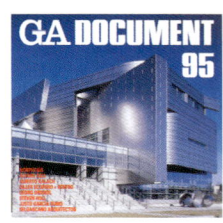

95
作品：モーフォシス ウェイン・ライマン・モース合衆国裁判所、ヒポ・アルプ・アドリア銀行本社／Á・シザ アデーガ・マイヨール／A・カラチ メキシコ国立図書館／ディラー・スコフィディオ＋レンフロ ボストン現代美術館／G・ドリエンドル ガルツィヒバーン・ベース・ターミナル／セルガス・カーノ・アルキテクトス バダホス会議場・劇場／他
Works: Morphosis Wayne Lyman Morse United States Courthouse; Á. Siza Adega Mayor; A. Kalach Public Library of Mexico; Diller Scofidio + Renfro Institute of Contemporary Art, Boston; G. Driendl Basis Terminal Galzigbahn; J. G. Rubio Casar de Cáceres Sub-Regional Bus Station; and others

120 pages, 78 in color ¥2,848

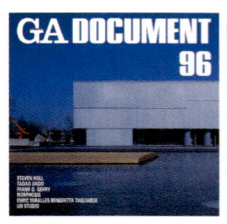

96
作品：S・ホール ネルソン＝アトキンス美術館／安藤忠雄＋日建設計 21_21 DESIGN SIGHT／F・O・ゲーリー IAC本社屋／モーフォシス アメリカ連邦ビル／E・ミラージェス・B・タグリアブエ エンリック・ミラージェス図書館／UNスタジオ 防御壕に載るティー・ハウス／UNスタジオ レリスタッド劇場
Works: S. Holl Nelson-Atkins Museum of Art; T. Ando + Nikken Sekkei 21_21 Design Sight; F. O. Gehry IAC Building; Morphosis United States Federal Building; E. Miralles B. Tagliabue Enric Miralles Public Library; UN Studio Tea House on Bunker; UN Studio Theater Lelystad

108 pages, 72 in color ¥2,848

97
特集：第15回〈現代世界の建築家〉展
Special Feature: "GA INTERNATIONAL 2007" Exhibition at GA Gallery

Tadao Ando, Coop Himmelblau, Peter Eisenman, Norman Foster, Frank O. Gehry, Zaha Hadid, Hiroshi Hara, Steven Holl, Arata Isozaki, Toyo Ito, Kengo Kuma, Daniel Libeskind, Fumihiko Maki, Mansilla + Tuñón, Morphosis, Jean Nouvel, OMA, Dominique Perrault, Renzo Piano, Richard Rogers, SANAA, Álvaro Siza, Yoshio Taniguchi, Bernard Tschumi, UN studio

132 pages, 72 in color ¥2,848

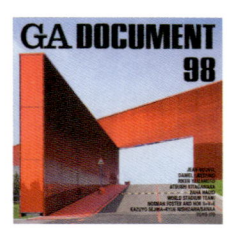

98
作品：J・ヌヴェル ブレンボ研究開発センター／D・リベスキンド ルネッサンスROM（王立オンタリオ美術館増築）／山本理顕 横須賀美術館／北川原温 KEYFOREST871228（キース・ヘリング美術館）／N・フォスター＆HOK S+V+E 国立ウェンブリー・スタジアム 展覧会：Z・ハディド アーキテクチャー＆デザイン
Works: J. Nouvel Brembo's Research and Development Center; D. Libeskind Renaissance ROM (Extension to the Royal Ontario Museum); R. Yamamoto Yokosuka Museum of Art; A. Kitagawara KEYFOREST871228 (Keith Haring Museum); SANAA 'De Kunstline' Theater and Cultural Center, Almere; T. Ito Tama Art University Library
Exhibition: Zaha Hadid Architecture and Design

108 pages, 66 in color ¥2,848

表記価格に消費税は含まれておりません。

99 SPECIAL ISSUE: ZAHA HADID
世界各地で精力的にプロジェクトを手がけるザハ・ハディド。彼女へのインタヴューをはじめ、現在進行中の40にものぼるプロジェクト、および家具・プロダクトや展覧会の模様を一挙に紹介します。
Interview: Interview with Zaha Hadid
40 Projects: MAXXI: National Museum of XXI Century Arts; Sheikh Zayed Bridge; Maritime Terminal Salerno; New Station Napoli Afragola; London Aquatics Centre; Dubai Financial Market; Abu Dhabi Performing Arts Center; and others
Furniture: Swarm Chandelier; Louis Vuitton Icone Bag; Z.Car; and others
Exhibition: Great Utopias; Mind Zone, Millennium Dome; and others

204 pages, 108 in color ¥3,800

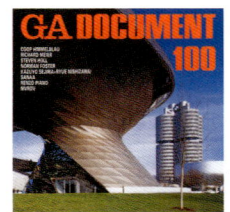

100
作品：コープ・ヒンメルブラウ BMWヴェルト、ミュンヘン美術アカデミー、アクロン美術館／R・マイヤー アルプ美術館／S・ホール ニューヨーク大学哲学科インテリア改修／N・フォスター スミソニアン・インスティテューション、ロバート＆アーレン・コゴッド・コート／妹島和世＋西沢立衛／SANAA ニューミュージアム、ニューヨーク
Works: Coop Himmelblau BMW Welt, Academy of Fine Arts Munich, Akron Art Museum; R. Meier Arp Museum; S. Holl Interior Renovation of New York University, Department of Philosophy; N. Foster Robert and Arlene Kogod Courtyard, Smithsonian Institution; SANAA New Museum of Contemporary Art

108 pages, 72 in color ¥2,848

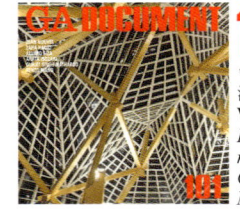

101
作品：J・ヌヴェル ミニメトロ／Z・ハディド ノルドパーク・ケーブル鉄道／Á・シザ ヴィアナ・ド・カステロの図書館／Á・シザ ゴンドマールの多目的パヴィリオン／磯崎新 深圳文化中心／G・S・マタロー プラタマ血液バンク／R・ピアノ ニューヨーク・タイムズ・ビル
Works: J. Nouvel Minimetro; Z. Hadid Nordpark Cable Railway; Á. Siza Viana do Castelo Library; Á. Siza Gondmar Multipurpose Pavilion; A. Isozaki Shenzhen Cultural Centre; G. S. Matharoo Prathama Blood Bank; R. Piano The New York Times Building

108 pages, 72 in color ¥2,848

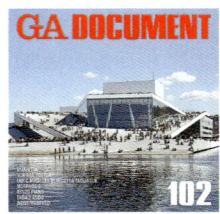

102
作品：スノヘッタ オスロ新オペラハウス／N・フォスター 北京国際空港、ターミナル3/T3／E・ミラージェス・B・タグリアブエ ガス・ナチュラル新本社／モーフォシス マドリッド公営集合住宅／R・ピアノ 現代美術館／BCAM（LACMA増築第一期）／ウェイス／マンフレディ シアトル美術館、オリンピック彫刻公園／他
Works: Snøhetta New Opera House Oslo; N. Foster Beijing Capital International Airport, Terminal 3/T3; Morphosis Madrid Social Housing; R. Piano Broad Contemporary Art Museum/BCAM; T.Ando Interfaculty Initiative in Information Studies Fukutake Hall; and others

108 pages, 72 in color ¥2,848

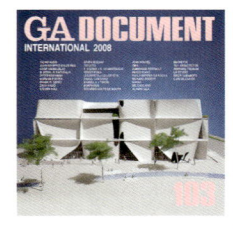

103
特集：第16回〈現代世界の建築家〉展
Special Feature: "GA INTERNATIONAL 2008" Exhibition at GA Gallery

T. Ando, J. N. Baldeweg, Coop Himmelblau, B. Doshi + R. Kathpalia, P. Eisenman, N. Foster, F. O. Gehry, Z. Hadid, S. Holl, A. Isozaki, T. Ito, K. Kojima + K. Akamatsu/CAt, K. Kuma, Legorreta + Legorreta, D. Libeskind, Mansilla + Tuñón, Morphosis, E. S. de Moura, J. Nouvel, OMA, D. Perrault, R. Piano, P, M. da Rocha, R. Rogers, SANAA, Selgascano, Á. Siza, Snøhetta, TEN Arquitectos, B. Tschumi, UN Studio, R. Yamamoto, C. Zapata

168 pages, 90 in color ¥2,848

104
作品：Á・シザ イベレ・カマルゴ財団美術館／Z・ハディド サラゴサ・ブリッジ・パヴィリオン／Z・ハディド モバイル・アート（シャネル・コンテンポラリー・アート・コンテイナー）／D・ペロー スカイ・ホテル／R・オオタケ ホテル・ユニーク／E・ミラージェス・B・タグリアブエ ヴィゴ大学、教員棟
Works: Á. Siza Museum for Iberê Camargo Foundation; Z. Hadid Zaragoza Bridge Pavilion; Z. Hadid Mobile Art—Chanel Contemporary Art Container; D. Perrault Sky Hotel; R. Ohtake Hotel Unique; E. Miralles B. Tagliabue Rectorate Building, University of Vigo

新刊

108 pages, 66 in color ¥2,848